CELEBRATING
SOUTHERN
APPALACHIAN
FOOD

CELEBRATING
SOUTHERN APPALACHIAN FOOD

Recipes & Stories from Mountain Kitchens

JIM CASADA AND TIPPER PRESSLEY

AMERICAN PALATE

Published by American Palate
A Division of The History Press
Charleston, SC
www.historypress.com

First published 2023

Manufactured in the United States

ISBN 9781467152778

Library of Congress Control Number: 2022950049

Notice: The information in this book is true and complete to the best of our knowledge. It is offered without guarantee on the part of the authors or The History Press. The authors and The History Press disclaim all liability in connection with the use of this book.

For Pap and Granny, my parents, who taught me to love the foodways of the Appalachian Mountains.
—Tipper Pressley

In fond memory of three of the finest cooks
I have ever known—my paternal grandmother,
Minnie Price Casada; my mother, Anna Lou Moore Casada; and my late wife,
Ann Fox Casada. Collectively, they were my culinary compass as well as the
providers of the vast majority of the finest meals I have ever eaten.
—Jim Casada

CONTENTS

Contents

ACKNOWLEDGEMENTS

Our gratitude goes out to members of our respective families who have, knowingly and otherwise, contributed to this book. Over the course of many generations and through the gifted hands of countless cooks, they have loved the mountain setting, garnered a living from its soil and gifted us with a grand inheritance. Their legacy, rich in tradition and taste as well as being redolent of the folkways of mountain food, is one we strive earnestly to honor and perpetuate in this book's pages.

In addition, we want to express appreciation to Jason Brady, university library specialist in special and digital collections at Western Carolina University's Hunter Library, and Mike Aday, archivist for the Great Smoky Mountains National Park, for gracious assistance in not only locating vintage photographs but also optimizing them for publication. Don Casada has generously shared his knowledge of the region and his photographic skills. We are also indebted to Kate Jenkins and Zoe Ames with The History Press. They have provided stellar guidance, admirably prompt responses and welcome expertise at every step along the way.

Finally, we both acknowledge a deep and enduring debt to those countless southern Appalachian culinary wizards who have practiced and perpetuated the region's foodways over many generations. They are our lamplights and lodestones reminding us of the deeply rooted truth of a venerable historian's adage: "You can't know where you are going if you don't know where you've been." We can only hope these pages are, in some measure, worthy of where we have been as we travel the path they have laid for us.

INTRODUCTION

Both of us come from families with roots in the Appalachian South running back over many generations. In our case, the geographical setting happens to be the mountains of southwestern North Carolina, but the culinary folkways characterizing our respective lives have a far broader reach. With a delightful spicing of local variations in cooking practices, favorite dishes and the most common crops and foodstuffs, along with other localized minor differences, they have a considerable degree of similarity across a wide region. That is what the recipes in the pages that follow endeavor to capture—the flavors and flair, traditions and tastes of southern Appalachia.

Several things need to be made clear at the outset. Neither of us is a culinary professional in any sense. We have never darkened the doors of a classroom at a culinary institute or higher learning establishment as students. Nor have we cooked in restaurants or similar settings, unless you count weekly kitchen stints for one summer in a tourist resort town in the Smokies where Jim substituted for the cook, who regularly was too hungover to work the day following receipt of his paycheck. Our training comes strictly in the practical fashion that has long typified the region's cooking. Namely, what we know (and most of the recipes we share) derives from training by family forebears along with an essential and irreplaceable aspect of cooking, as those from whom we learned might have put it: practical, firsthand "doings in the kitchen."

Tipper does have some background experience as a former teacher of cooking classes at the John C. Campbell Folk School along with hundreds of posts and videos on the two mediums through which she shares her expertise, her *Blind Pig & the Acorn* blog and *Celebrating Appalachia* YouTube channel. While neither is devoted exclusively to cooking, food constitutes one of the central features of both offerings. The former appears daily through the year and has done so for well over a decade, while the latter, which is of more recent vintage, is offered several times each week. It, too, explores food preparation, along with culinary folkways and closely related subjects such as gardening, on a frequent basis. She is also the author of a small e-cookbook featuring some of her all-time favorite recipes.

Jim, although he has enjoyed cooking all his life and even did a bit of kitchen work during the aforementioned summertime stint in a restaurant, became involved in culinary communication in a significant fashion when he became a full-time freelance writer focusing on hunting, fishing and the natural world. That led to a number of cookbooks coauthored with his late wife, Ann. More recently, he has written about the manner in which various aspects of food—gardening; care of livestock and utilization of the fruits of such efforts in the form of eggs, dairy products and meat; preservation of foodstuffs; and cooking—have been shaping factors in his life. That includes a regular column in *Smoky Mountain Living* magazine, scores of contributions of recipes and food lore to the *Sporting Classics Daily* blog and, most significantly, his autobiographical *Fishing for Chickens: A Smokies Food Memoir*. He has also given talks on cooking and done demonstrations, mostly involving wild game, for sportsmen's groups, hunt clubs and similar gatherings.

The subject areas and recipes in the pages that follow represent a cross section of what we have eaten and prepared all our respective lives. They also typify traditional Appalachian dishes and focus on foods, whether from the garden or nature's larder, that have formed the essence of regional diet over many generations. You will find numerous recipes covering foods lying at the heart of Appalachian foodways, the "corn and taters," as well as "maters and other garden truck," found on mountain tables throughout the year. Corn, a key crop not only for humans but also for barnyard beasts and fowl, is given prominent attention at the outset, while a panoply of recipes for desserts in the form of cakes, pies, cookies, jellies and more pay ample recognition to the prominence sweets have always played in regional diet. Altogether, close to three hundred recipes celebrate the enduring and endearing heritage that is cooking in Appalachia.

If this was a highly formalized cookbook focusing on haute cuisine and bandying about terms such as *foie gras, au vin, reduction* and *remoulade,* this would be the point where we wished readers *bon appétit.* Instead, given the nature of this book's contents and the region of its coverage, perhaps a thought from Jim's beloved paternal grandfather is more appropriate. Whenever Grandpa Joe sat down at a table laden with lovingly prepared foodstuffs from Grandma Minnie's kitchen, he would bless the food in a truly heartfelt and meaningful fashion. He always concluded with the same words: "You'uns see what's before you. Eat hearty!"

Following his line of thinking, "you'uns" see what is available in terms of recipes recognizing a regional heritage rich in the joy of good food taken from the good earth and prepared in loving and luscious fashion. We encourage you to sample and savor the wide array of foodstuffs in the pages that follow, and as you do so, it is our genuine hope that you will celebrate the wonders of the Appalachian South's food folkways in a manner bringing an ample measure of culinary pleasure.

GLOSSARY OF
SOUTHERN APPALACHIAN FOOD TERMS

Both of us use—conversationally in general and especially when talking of cooking—traditional food terms that lie outside the normal vocabulary of cookbooks and cuisine. Provided below is a glossary of some of the more common usages from the region, many of them encountered in these pages.

arsh tater—Irish potato.

bait—A mess or ample quantity, often preceded by the word big. "We had us a big bait of turnip greens and cornbread for supper."

bile, biled—Boil, boiled.

blinked—Milk that has spoiled. "You need to check on that milk to be sure it isn't blinked."

butter—A sweet fruit preparation, as opposed to the dairy product, made with either molasses or sugar and often used to spread on biscuits or loaf bread.

cannery—An outbuilding used to store canned goods and, often, cured pork.

cathead biscuit—A large biscuit, equivalent in size to the head of a cat; a biscuit cut from dough using the open end of a tin can.

cowcumber—A colloquialism for *cucumber*.

cracklings—Crisp tidbits left when pork fat is rendered into lard.

cushaw (*or* kushaw)—A large winter squash with a taste resembling that of pumpkin.

dash—A synonym for *pinch*; a tiny addition to a recipe.

dinner—The meal eaten at midday.

dope—A soda pop or carbonated beverage. The word likely derives from the fact that cocaine was used in the original Coca-Cola.

drib (*also* dribs and drabs)—A small portion; a little bit. "She added melted butter to the batter in dribs and drabs."

drop—Seldom used in the literal sense; instead, a drop in a recipe means the addition of a small amount.

dusting—A small amount, usually associated with some foodstuff that is fine or powdery. For example, you might top a cake with a dusting of powdered sugar.

fatback—Salted meat, widely used in Appalachian cooking for seasoning. Synonyms or near synonyms, although the meat might come from different sections of a hog, include streaked meat, middling meat, streak o' lean, salt pork, pork belly, seasoning meat and others.

flumlolly—A small biscuit made from the dough remaining after full-size biscuits have been cut out. Also known as a baby biscuit.

fruit—Apples loom so large in importance as a foodstuff that they are sometimes simply called *fruit*.

glob—A considerable quantity. "She always added a glob of butter to her cobblers."

grabble—To dig out new potatoes gently without disturbing the entire hill.

greasy beans—A particular type of green bean, so named because of its slick appearance.

hickory chickens—Morel mushrooms.

hint—An expression for a minute quantity. "What made that pot likker was just a hint of red pepper."

hoecake—Fried cornbread.

June apples—Any of a number of varieties of apples that ripen in midsummer rather than autumn.

kilt—Killed; primarily used to describe the result of pouring hot grease over fresh lettuce or other greens as a dressing.

larrup (*or* larruping)—Exceptionally tasty; sometimes used with the main ingredient: i.e., berry larrup.

leather—Dried version of a variety of fruits.

leather britches—Dried green beans.

little hominy—Grits.

long sweetening—Honey, molasses or sorghum syrup.

look—To check a foodstuff, such as dried beans, carefully to remove unwanted particles.

lump—A word normally used in connection with some specification of size. "At this point, add a lump of lard the size of a banty's egg."

made—Usually applied to a crop that has matured or reached the harvest stage.

mangos—Sweet peppers.

maypops—Fruit of the passionflower; also known as wild apricots.

merkels (miracles)—Morel mushrooms.

mess—A hearty serving or servings. An adequate quantity for a meal. "We had a mess of turnip greens and pone of cornbread for supper."

mite—A quantitative expression usually connected with overdoing some ingredient or failing to include enough of it. "There's a mite too much pepper in this stew for my taste," or "A mite more sugar would have made that rhubarb pie better."

molasses—Colloquial term widely used to describe sorghum syrup, as opposed to true molasses made from sugarcane.

nubbin—Literally, a small cob of corn; in a food context, a small amount.

okry—A common pronunciation of the word *okra*.

partridge (*also* pottige)—A colloquialism for ruffed grouse.

passel—A large quantity. "It took a passel of taters to feed that hungry bunch."

pinch—A small amount. See also *scrimption, scootch, skiver, smattering, smidgen* and *tetch*.

poke—A wild vegetable eaten when its sprouts first appear in the spring.

pole beans—Any type of climbing bean.

pone—Cornbread cooked in a round skillet.

pot likker—The broth from cooking cabbage, greens or other vegetables.

put up—To preserve food for later use; usually, though not always, refers to canning.

redeye gravy—Grease left after frying ham, usually mixed with water or coffee and used as gravy.

roasting ears—Fresh corn.

run—A single batch of canned goods, kraut or the like. "We canned a run of green beans this morning."

saucered (*or* sassered)—Coffee or hot tea poured in a saucer to cool before drinking.

sawmill gravy (*or*, *rarely*, sawdust gravy). A hearty gravy using cornmeal, lard or grease from streaked meat and water. It was common fare in logging camps, hence the name.

scootch—A tiny amount.

scrimption (*or* skimption)—A small amount.

short sweetening—Brown or white sugar.

skiver—A small portion of something; often used for snow but also for cooking ingredients.

smattering—A small or inadequate amount. "There was just a smattering of cracklin's in that cornbread."

smidgen—A small amount; synonym for *pinch*.

smokehouse—A building used to store and smoke pork as a part of the curing process.

soodlin—An indeterminate portion; usually with a helping of food. "Would you care for a soodlin more preserves?"

soup beans—A general term for dried beans most commonly applied to pintos, October beans and navy beans.

sugar—In addition to a sweetening agent, often used to describe a kiss.

supper—The evening meal.

sweet milk—Whole milk.

tad—A small amount.

taste—Enough of an ingredient for its flavor to be discernible. "I like to add just a taste of allspice to my pumpkin pie."

tetch—A touch or very small amount. "That stew needs just a tetch more salt."

tommytoes—Small tomatoes sometimes known as cherry tomatoes.

vittles—Victuals or foodstuffs.

work off—Allow kraut or pickles to ferment; also used to describe the process of making hard cider or moonshine.

yard birds—Any free-ranging domestic fowl, although most commonly applied to chickens.

Chapter 1

MAKIN'S FROM CORN AND CORNMEAL

THE SOUL OF APPALACHIAN COOKING

I f bread lies at the heart of Appalachian culinary ways, baked goods using cornmeal can sort of be reckoned the mother church of the bread family. Corn as a crop has always been ideally suited to the region's geography. A patch can be grown almost anywhere there is a piece of cleared ground, from steep hillsides to fertile river bottomland and all types of topography in between. Moreover, corn is a crop featuring exceptional versatility. Freshly picked corn in the form of roasting ears is a summertime dietary treat that can, with successive plantings, be enjoyed over a time span of as long as three months.

The primary usage of corn, however, has always come in its fully matured, dried form. It is ideally suited for human consumption not only thanks to its taste but also because the grain stores well (corn with the shucks left intact will, if protected from moisture and pests such as rats and weevils, keep almost indefinitely). Historically, it could be ground in small quantities in simple tub mills as well as larger, more complex overshot waterwheel operations. This translated to ready production of meal in a process that was appreciably less complex than the milling of other grains such as wheat, rye or buckwheat. With corn, there was minimal waste. Leavings from poorly formed or inferior ears, sometimes called nubbins, served admirably as scratch feed for chickens or as supplemental food for hogs in the fattening-up times of autumn.

Corn fodder fed livestock and, when stacked in shocks, provided a makeshift yet eminently practical means of food storage to protect long-keeping vegetables such as pumpkins, potatoes and cabbage from freezing during the depths of winter's cold. Cobs from shelled corn could be fashioned

A bunch of boys, hoes in hand, ready to get busy with weed chopping in a corn patch. *Courtesy of Hunter Library, Western Carolina University.*

into jug stoppers, carved to make pipes or soaked in kerosene to provide a dandy fire starter. Corn was, in short, an ideal crop, and that holds true even without venturing into the fabled traditions associated with the grain in its liquid form. The recipes that follow are but a slender sampling of the ways in which it can be prepared, and all these focus on its use in the making of bread. Other usages for corn as a fresh vegetable occur later in the book.

Of the myriad methods for using corn, baking it in what was normally called pone was the most common. Yet the word *cornbread* embraced an array of preparations, with ingredients varying quite remarkably. An example of that consideration is provided by the methods our families have used, and our respective recipes for it provide two illustrations of how to prepare this most traditional of Appalachian foodstuffs.

Of course, cornbread merely forms a starting point for the many baked variations—fritters, hushpuppies, dodgers, corn cakes (cooked on a griddle just like pancakes), etc.—that can be made from cornmeal. Then there are so many things you can add to the batter—cracklings, jalapeños or other "hot" stuff for Mexican cornbread, corn kernels and the like. What is offered here is nothing more than a small sampling of the unending delights afforded by cornmeal.

Tipper's Cornbread

Cornbread is the quintessential bread of Appalachia. Although batter recipes vary, the key to making traditional cornbread is to use a preheated cast-iron pan for baking.

Bacon fat or lard
2 cups self-rising white cornmeal
1 egg, beaten
¼ cup vegetable oil
1 ⅓ cups milk

A perfectly browned pone of cornbread hot from a cast-iron skillet. *Tipper Pressley.*

Grease cast-iron pan liberally with bacon fat or lard. Place in cold oven and preheat to 475 degrees. Place 2 cups cornmeal in mixing bowl. Combine egg, oil and milk and then pour into bowl with cornmeal and mix thoroughly. Carefully remove heated pan from oven and add batter. Bake for 20 minutes or until done.

NOTE: Plain cornmeal can also be used by adding 1 teaspoon of baking soda and 1 teaspoon of salt.

TIP: Sprinkling the hot pan with cornmeal before adding your batter will make an even crisper crust.

—Tipper Pressley

Cornbread the Casada Way

"My way" simply means cornbread as it has long been made in my family, and with slight variations, I think you'll find the recipe that follows is fairly standard among the folks of southern Appalachia. Some key points, before we even get to the recipe, are:

1. *Cook in a well-greased cast-iron skillet.*
2. *Grease the skillet with a piece of streaked meat or bacon before you pour in the batter.*

3. Use stone-ground cornmeal. Store-bought stuff is ground at too high a rate, and heat hurts its flavor. Also, if you like a bit of crunch in your cornbread, and I do, stone-ground meal, even if sifted, has more "body" to it.

4. Use buttermilk, not sweet milk. This recipe makes just the right size pone for a standard 9-inch cast-iron skillet. A frequently uttered adage holds that "yellow corn is for critters and white corn for folks," but my personal preference is for yellow cornmeal.

1 extra-large egg
1 ⅓ cups buttermilk
¼ cup bacon drippings
2 cups stone-ground yellow cornmeal
Cracklings (optional)
⅓ cup frozen corn kernels (optional)

Preheat your oven to 400 degrees. Mix all the ingredients in a large bowl and whisk until thoroughly blended. Place the pan—well seasoned by rubbing in a bit of the bacon grease or by running a piece of streaked meat across it after the pan is hot—in the oven for a few minutes. Then take out and pour the batter into the pan, return to the oven and cook until golden brown.

Gritting corn from the cob.
Jim Casada.

TIPS:

1. If you have access to cracklings, add a handful to the batter when you stir it up and cut back just a tad on the bacon drippings.

2. For a bit more moisture and a nice texture surprise, add ⅓ cup of frozen corn kernels (thaw them in advance) to the batter.

3. When you remove the cooked pone from the oven, place a couple of pats of butter atop it and, as they melt, spread them across the crust.

—Jim Casada

Cornbread and Milk

Since cornbread is so common in the mountains of Appalachia, a need to use leftover bread often arises. One of the most popular ways to use any remaining cornbread is to mix it with milk. Fill a glass with crumbled cornbread and pour either sweet milk or buttermilk over it.

A glass of cornbread and milk, often served as supper in the Appalachians.
Tipper Pressley.

NOTES:

1. Onions, salt and pepper can be added to the glass for a richer meal.

2. Honey and other sweeteners can be added to make the dish more of a sweet dessert.

TIP: Cornbread and milk makes a great breakfast.

—Tipper Pressley

Cornbread Salad

Another wonderful way to use leftover cornbread is to make a big bowl of cornbread salad. The recipe couldn't be easier. The ingredients can be changed according to what you have on hand. The amounts can be adjusted to fit the amount of cornbread you have, as well.

Cornbread
Onion, chopped
Tomato, diced
1 (8-ounce) can beans (pinto and kidney work well)
1 handful shredded cheese
Your favorite dressing (ranch works especially well)

Crumble cornbread in a large bowl. Add onion, tomato, beans and cheese, season to taste and dress salad.

Peppers, radishes, cucumbers and other vegetables can be added.

The ingredients can be layered in a glass bowl for a pretty presentation, but I prefer to mix them all together.

NOTE: The salad is better after it marries in the fridge overnight.

TIP: The salad makes a perfect quick weekday supper.

—Tipper Pressley

Hushpuppies

Aunt Mag Williams, a wonderful Black cook from my youth, always had piping hot hushpuppies (and slaw) to go with fish. I have no idea how she made them, but as is true of this recipe, they did have as essential ingredients cornmeal and onion. She often, though not always, included corn kernels in her batter. This was in the summertime, when fresh corn on the cob was readily available.

1 ½ cups cornmeal
1 cup self-rising flour
½ teaspoon seasoned garlic salt
½ cup chopped onion (or scallions)
1 (8-ounce) can cream-style corn
1 egg
1 cup whole milk
Cooking oil

Combine the cornmeal, flour and garlic salt in a bowl and mix well. Beat the onion, corn, eggs and milk in a separate bowl and add them to the dry ingredients. Place the mixture in the freezer to cool while you heat cooking oil to 375 degrees in a deep fryer. Drop teaspoons of the batter, just a few hushpuppies at a time, into the hot oil. Cook until golden brown, turning to cook evenly on all sides. Makes about 30 large hushpuppies.

NOTE: Recipe can be doubled (or expanded by other multiples).

—Jim Casada

Pap's Gritted Bread

1 ½ cups grated corn (if using really fresh corn, allow some of the milk to drain out)
⅔ cup all-purpose flour
1 teaspoon salt
½ teaspoon baking soda
1 teaspoon baking powder
1 egg, beaten
1 cup sweet milk or buttermilk
2 tablespoons bacon grease (optional, especially if using buttermilk)

Combine all ingredients together. The batter should resemble pancake batter. If needed, additional flour or milk can be added to thicken or thin. Cook in hot greased frying pan as you would pancakes or pour into hot, well-greased frying pan and bake at 450 degrees until done.

A skillet of gritted bread. *Tipper Pressley.*

NOTE: This recipe works best with corn that has begun to harden slightly.

TIP: Gritted bread is wonderful served with soup beans or with a smear of jelly.

—Tipper Pressley

Cornmeal Mush

Cornmeal mush makes a tasty breakfast cereal and can also be allowed to set up and sliced for frying, giving two options.

2 cups water
Pinch salt
1 cup cornmeal
Butter
Honey, syrup or sugar

Bring water to a boil; add salt; slowly add cornmeal, stirring constantly to prevent lumping. Continue cooking and stirring until thick and creamy. Serve with butter, sugar, honey or whatever pleases you.

NOTE: Cornmeal mush is called polenta in other cultures.

Fried cornmeal mush. *Tipper Pressley.*

TIP: Pour mush into a bread pan or other container and allow it to set up overnight. Remove from pan and slice; fry in hot grease until brown. Slices can be dipped into flour or egg to form a browner crust when fried.

—Tipper Pressley

Chestnut Dressing

½ cup butter or margarine
I cup finely chopped celery
I cup finely chopped onion
I cup cooked, chopped chestnuts (you can substitute pecans)
6–8 cups cornbread crumbs (homemade is better)
I egg, beaten
2 (or more) cups chicken or turkey broth
Salt and pepper to taste (those who like sage can add it as well,
but keep in mind it has a dominating flavor)

Melt butter in skillet and sauté celery, onion and nuts. Cook slowly over low heat for 10 minutes; stir frequently, as this burns easily. Add to cornbread crumbs in mixing bowl. Add beaten egg and broth, mixing well. Dressing must be *very* moist; add more broth if needed. Season to taste with salt, pepper and sage (omit sage if you wish, which I do). Bake in casserole dish at 350 degrees for 30 to 45 minutes or until golden brown.

TIP: Leftover dressing is just as tasty as when the preparation has just come from the oven, and it can be reheated for a side dish, adorned with gravy or mixed with chopped-up chicken or turkey and fried as cakes.

—Jim Casada

Corn Pudding

⅔ cup all-purpose flour
½ cup cornmeal
2 tablespoons sugar
1 tablespoon baking powder
¼ teaspoon salt
1 can cream-style corn
1 can whole-kernel corn (do not drain)
1 small container (8 ounces) sour cream
1 stick butter

Mix all ingredients—except butter—in a bowl. Pour into greased casserole dish. Melt butter and pour on top; do not stir. Bake uncovered at 350 degrees for 50 minutes or until light brown and set in the middle.

NOTE: This recipe makes a good bread replacement.

TIP: A box of Jiffy Cornbread mix may be substituted for the first five ingredients.

—Tipper Pressley

Cornpone Pie
This recipe is really just a variation on time-tested approaches to making cornbread in a fashion that basically becomes, if not an entire meal, at least the key dish. In a sense, it is a derivative of both cracklin' cornbread and cornbread with soup beans. The ingredients vary a bit from those traditional standards, and the meat and beans provide a double dose of protein.

1 extra-large egg
1 ⅓ cups buttermilk
¼ cup bacon drippings
2 cups stone-ground yellow cornmeal
⅓ cup frozen corn kernels (optional; thaw them in advance)
½ pound 80 percent lean hamburger or a comparable amount of venison ground
with bacon ends or pork fat
1 medium onion, diced
1 can pinto beans (drained) or 1 ½ cups previously cooked pintos

Mix egg, buttermilk, bacon drippings, cornmeal and corn kernels in a large bowl and whisk until thoroughly blended. (Or use your regular recipe for cornbread, leaving out the cooking oil.) Set batter aside (something I also do when making regular cornbread) while browning ½ pound of 80 percent lean hamburger or a comparable amount of ground venison (if you use the latter, mix in a bit of bacon or pork fat) in a skillet along with a diced sweet onion.

When the meat is fully browned, pour the pintos into the cornmeal batter, add the meat-and-onion mix, stir just enough to mix completely and pour into a preheated baking dish or well-greased cast-iron skillet. Bake at 400 degrees until done.

—Jim Casada

GRITS AND HOMINY

Grits aren't made from cornmeal, but along with hominy, they fall into the category of dishes made from dried corn as opposed to its standard fresh vegetable usage. Accordingly, they seem a better fit here than in the vegetable recipes portion of the book. They are a standard source of dietary starch falling in the same category as breads. While most often served at breakfast, they can be an accompaniment to any meal.

An Indian woman preparing corn for a run of hominy. *Courtesy of the National Park Service.*

Fried Grits

When allowed to cool after having been cooked, grits readily congeal. To enjoy fried grits, cook an extra batch when you are having them as a breakfast dish and place the surplus, while still warm enough to flow, in a baking dish or rectangular cake pan. Keep in refrigerator until ready to use, then cut into serving-size sections. Lightly oil a skillet and fry the grits cakes, turning once. Easy and scrumptious.

—Jim Casada

Chapter 2

CATHEAD BISCUITS, BISCUIT BREAD AND MORE WONDERS FROM WHEAT

n Appalachia, biscuits have traditionally been breakfast bread, although leftovers could be used at any time. They were also something to be baked whenever gravy was going to be on the menu. Most of the time, in day-to-day diet, though, cornbread ruled the culinary roost. Biscuits weren't quite in the position of rarefied "special" treats, but they didn't have the same "common fare" billing as cornbread. Occasionally, usually when time was at a premium, cooks would take a shortcut and bake biscuit bread. There was no difference in the dough; it was just that when a kitchen wizard didn't have time or want to be troubled by the final step of patting out or cutting individual biscuits, they took a shortcut. They simply put their kneaded dough in a pan or atop a cookie sheet. It would be served as a whole piece, and you just broke off or cut a chunk, much like was done with cornbread.

Regular biscuits, properly made, were a source of quiet but significant pride among Appalachian cooks. Few words of praise were more welcome than statements such as "Her biscuits are so light they almost float on air," "That woman's biscuits rise like the morning sun" or "Now that's a sho' 'nuff cathead biscuit." The latter description applied to a really large biscuit, and many cooks had their own special device or method of cutting a biscuit of considerable size. Whatever descriptions might be used in connection with biscuits, they were a step or two up the ladder from cornbread in much the same fashion chicken ranked above pork on the meat scale. Biscuits may or may not have been daily fare, but they invariably graced the table when the local preacher, out-of-town family or special guests came to eat.

Biscuits kneaded, patted, cut and ready to bake. *Tipper Pressley.*

Grandma Casada's Biscuits and Biscuit Bread

In this particular case, I'll have to confess that I have no idea how Grandma Minnie worked her culinary magic with biscuits. I just know they were always perfect—light, fluffy, shaped by hand and big enough to hold a fried egg from Grandpa Joe's chickens without white sticking out over the edges. Often, if she was in a hurry, Grandma wouldn't make individual biscuits. She'd just get the dough ready and put it in a loaf pan for baking as biscuit bread. The taste was the same, and when it came to biscuits and gravy, it was just the ticket.

While I don't remember Grandma's biscuit recipe, and Momma always left this aspect of food preparation to her, this is pretty much what was involved, and it's also the approach used by my coauthor for her "never fail" biscuits (see her recipe following this one).

2 cups self-rising flour
1 to 1½ cups heavy cream

Mix flour and cream well and knead once or twice. Cut out biscuits from the resulting dough and place on an ungreased baking sheet. Bake at 450 degrees for 10 minutes or until a light golden brown on top.

About all that then remains is to slather with butter and your favorite jam, jelly or syrup as biscuit adornment. When an advertising genius for an old-time cane syrup called Dixie Dew said it "gives a biscuit a college education," he knew whereof he spoke. Alternately, cut the cathead open and apply plenty of gravy. Let out your belt two notches and get busy with your trencherman duties!

—Jim Casada

Cream Biscuits

2 cups self-rising flour (I prefer White Lily)
1 cup heavy whipping cream

Using a ratio of 2 to 1 makes this recipe easily decreased or increased depending on need. Mix flour and cream together and turn out onto a lightly floured surface. Kneed once or twice until mixture comes together; add a little flour, if needed. Flatten dough out with your hand or a rolling pin and cut with a biscuit cutter or glass. Place biscuits on baking pan and bake at 450 degrees for about 10 to 12 minutes or until golden brown.

TIP: This recipe can also be used to make baked hand pies.

—Tipper Pressley

Cheese Biscuits

Cheese biscuits finished to a golden turn. *Tipper Pressley.*

Make cream biscuit recipe, add a good handful of grated cheddar cheese and sprinkle garlic powder to taste. Mix well. Drop batter by spoonfuls onto an ungreased baking sheet. Bake at 450 degrees for 10 to 12 minutes or until golden brown.

TIP: After removing the biscuits from the oven, brush melted butter on top for more decadence.

—Tipper Pressley

Baked Hand Pies

Cream biscuit dough
Applesauce or your favorite fruit preserve

Make cream biscuit recipe. Take a small amount of batter; on a floured surface, roll the ball out into a circular shape. Place a tablespoon of applesauce, or your favorite fruit preserve, in the middle of the circle. Fold the dough over and seal the edges by crimping with a fork or your fingers to keep all that sweet goodness inside. Poke a few holes in

Baked hand pies. *Tipper Pressley.*

the top to allow steam to escape. Place on greased baking sheet. Bake at 400 degrees for 15 to 20 minutes or until done, and you have a very tasty treat. Hand pies make a dandy dessert, snack or breakfast.

TIP: A small saucer can be used to trace out a more precise circle.

—Tipper Pressley

Buttermilk Biscuit Bread

2 teaspoons bacon drippings (or lard)
2 cups self-rising flour
¼ cup cold butter, cut into cubes
1 ½ to 2 cups buttermilk

Add bacon drippings or lard to an 8-inch cast-iron frying pan and place pan in cold oven. Preheat oven to 400 degrees. Place flour in bowl and cut in butter until it resembles coarse crumbs. Add buttermilk to flour mixture. The batter will be very moist but shouldn't be runny. Pour batter into hot cast-iron pan. Spread the dough evenly over the bottom of the pan. Bake for 20 to 25 minutes or until the top is golden brown. Remove from oven and flip bread out onto a cooling rack or plate. Slice or break off and serve.

TIP: Baking dough in a piping hot frying pan gives the outside a wonderful chewy crust. The buttermilk adds a nice whang that goes perfectly with butter and honey.

NOTES:
An old adage suggests, "Biscuits that are light are biscuits that are right." Certainly, cooks take pride in light, fluffy biscuits, and there are a number of tricks of the baking trade to help in that regard.

1. Sift your flour immediately before making your dough. It may not need sifting for the usual reason (the removal of coarse pieces), but the process adds air.
2. Nestle individual biscuits next to one another in the pan. That encourages baking upward rather than outward.
3. Use a cast-iron skillet as your baking dish. It cooks from the side as well as the bottom. Better still, employ a Dutch oven.
4. Do not twist your biscuit cutter. This sort of seals the sides of the biscuits and keeps them from rising as easily.

Bake at high temperatures (you'll notice that most of the recipes above suggest 450 degrees). That encourages rising.

—Tipper Pressley

Chapter 3
FANCY DOIN'S

OTHER BREADS AND BAKED GOODS

B aking has always been a center-stage affair in Appalachian cooking, and it extends far beyond the daily routines involving cornbread and biscuits. This chapter looks at a small but representative cross section of other types of baked goods along with a couple of stove-top preparations from batter. Some type of sweetening figures in every offering but the first, and even with pancakes, there's a traditional topping of syrup, honey, jam or jelly. In reality, there's no clear dividing line between the recipes here—other than the use of the name *bread* rather than *cake* or *pie*—and some of those found in the latter portion of the book devoted to desserts.

All sorts of sweet breads have long found a home in Appalachian kitchens. Vegetables such as zucchini and squash, fruits such as persimmons and bananas, pumpkins and other members of the winter squash family and many further options await blending with flour, eggs, perhaps nuts and suitable seasonings to produce a dessert bread: something to enjoy with breakfast or perhaps a midafternoon pick-me-up anointed with cream cheese.

Traditional Buttermilk Pancakes
Appalachian folks have long prepared various types of bread by cooking in a pan or on a griddle as opposed to oven baking. Griddle cakes, hoe cakes and flapjacks are but a few of many examples. One enduring favorite

A stack of buttermilk pancakes awaiting syrup or honey.
Tipper Pressley.

is pancakes, a traditional breakfast foodstuff topped with sorghum syrup, honey, maple syrup, jelly or jam and often viewed as a special treat. Store-bought flour produced especially for pancakes can be used, but if you have access to stone-ground buckwheat flour, try it in this recipe for a delightful difference in taste and texture (and buckwheat is gluten-free).

I egg
2 tablespoons vegetable oil, bacon grease or lard
2 cups pancake flour (quality of this type of flour can vary a great deal—one of the best is the buttermilk flour from Pearl Milling Company, an operation that formerly carried the Aunt Jemima brand name)
I ½ cups buttermilk

Preheat your griddle to 375 degrees (you can also use a cast-iron skillet, but it will not hold as many pancakes, and turning them is a bit more difficult). Mix ingredients in a bowl with a pour spout, using a whisk. Stir until well blended, and if necessary, add buttermilk to obtain desired batter consistency (it should pour readily but still have a modest degree of thickness). Pour sufficient portions of batter to make 4-inch pancakes atop your preheated griddle. Allow to cook for I ½ minutes and then flip and cook for I additional minute. Make sure pancakes are browned on both sides and fully done. This recipe makes a dozen pancakes and can be doubled or tripled for larger groups.

TIPS:
1. Pancakes warm over quite well in a microwave.
2. Add chocolate chips, blueberries, slices of banana, bits of peaches, pitted and chopped cherries or other treats to your batter. Alternatively, to make sure these are evenly distributed, incorporate them into the top of each pancake before turning it.
3. When serving, rather than topping pancakes with syrup, pour syrup into the bottom of a plate and place the pancakes atop it.

—Jim Casada

Black Walnut and Banana Bread

½ cup vegetable oil
1 cup sugar
2 eggs
2 cups very ripe bananas, mashed with a fork
2 cups flour
1 teaspoon salt
1 teaspoon baking soda
½ cup finely chopped black walnuts

Mix vegetable oil, sugar, eggs and bananas well. Add flour, salt, baking soda and walnuts and mix thoroughly. Place in greased loaf pan and bake at 350 degrees for 1 hour or in four small loaf pans for 40 minutes.

TIP: Ripe bananas can be frozen, and it is also often possible to pick them up in grocery stores at greatly reduced rates.

—Jim Casada

Pap's Sweet Bread

Lard
2 eggs
¼ cup butter
1 cup milk
2 teaspoons vanilla
¾ cup sugar
2 cups self-rising flour

Preheat your oven to 350. Heat two cast-iron pans on the stove; add a spoonful of lard to each. While the lard is melting, break two eggs in a mixing bowl. Next, divide butter in half, adding one half to each pan. Add milk to eggs and mix well; add vanilla and mix well. Once butter is melted, pour most of it into the milk-and-egg mixture and stir well. Pap said he liked to melt his butter in the frying pan because it's one less dish to wash. Next, add sugar to mixture and stir well. Add flour and stir until smooth. Divide batter equally between the two pans and place in the oven. Bake for 20 to 25 minutes or until golden brown. Frosting can be added to the bread, but our favorite way to eat it is straight out of the pan. Pap liked to open a can of Granny's peaches to eat with his.

—Tipper Pressley

Granny Gazzie's Gingerbread Cookies

2½ tablespoons lard or shortening
1 cup sorghum syrup
1 egg
1 teaspoon ginger
1 teaspoon cinnamon
1 teaspoon nutmeg
¼ cup milk
3 cups self-rising flour

Beat lard and syrup until well blended; add egg and beat well. Mix spices with flour. Alternately, add milk and flour to syrup mixture to make a soft dough. Using additional flour, roll out dough and cut into desired shapes. Bake at 350 degrees for 10 minutes or until done. Baking time will depend on thickness of cookie.

TIP: Use a toothpick to make simple designs on your cookies before baking.

—Tipper Pressley

Pumpkin Bread

2½ cups sugar
3 eggs
15 ounces cooked pumpkin

Tipper Pressley savoring a slice of freshly made pumpkin bread. *Corie Graddick.*

1 cup shortening
3 cups all-purpose flour
1 teaspoon salt
½ teaspoon baking soda
1 teaspoon baking powder
1 ¼ teaspoons cinnamon
1 teaspoon cloves
1 teaspoon nutmeg
1 teaspoon allspice
1 ½ cups black walnuts

Combine sugar, eggs, pumpkin and shortening. In a separate bowl, sift together flour, salt, baking soda, baking powder, cinnamon, cloves, nutmeg and allspice. Combine pumpkin mixture with sifted mixture. Stir in black walnuts. Pour into greased loaf pans and bake for an hour at 350 degrees.

NOTE: Other nuts may be used; pecans are especially good in this recipe.

—Jim Casada

Honey Nut Bread

2 cups flour
3 teaspoons baking powder
½ teaspoon salt
½ cup coarsely chopped nuts
1 egg, beaten
½ cup honey
½ cup milk
2 tablespoons melted butter

Sift dry ingredients and add nuts (pecans, English walnuts, black walnuts or even hickory nuts can be used). Combine beaten egg, honey, milk and melted butter; add to first mixture. Stir until ingredients are just moist. Bake in greased bread pan at 350 for 25 to 30 minutes or until done. Makes wonderful breakfast bread when sliced and toasted.

NOTE: Honey nut bread goes especially well with a smear of cream cheese.

—Tipper Pressley

Apple Bread
This apple bread is very tasty; it's perfect for breakfast or an evening snack.

2 cups flour
2 teaspoons baking powder
1 teaspoon cinnamon
¼ teaspoon nutmeg
1 teaspoon salt
½ cup softened butter
1 ½ cups sugar
2 eggs
2 cups finely shredded apples
½ cup chopped nuts (black walnuts are especially good)

Sift together flour, baking powder, cinnamon, nutmeg and salt and set aside. Cream butter and sugar until light. Add eggs one at a time, mixing well after each. Add flour mixture and apples alternately. Stir in walnuts. Spoon into a well-greased loaf pan or use parchment paper to line the pan. Bake at 350 degrees for 1 hour or until done. Cool in pan 10 minutes. Remove from pan and cool completely.

—Tipper Pressley

Zucchini Bread

3 eggs
2 cups sugar
1 cup oil
1 tablespoon lemon juice
3 cups all-purpose flour
1 teaspoon baking soda
1 teaspoon baking powder
1 teaspoon cinnamon
2 cups grated zucchini
1 cup nuts

A loaf of pecan-studded zucchini bread. *Tipper Pressley.*

Beat eggs and sugar; add oil and lemon juice. Sift together flour and remaining dry ingredients; add to egg mixture. Mix well. Stir in zucchini and nuts. Bake in greased loaf pans at 325 degrees for 55 to 60 minutes or until done.

TIP: Pecan halves can be laid on top of the loaves for extra visual appeal.

—Jim Casada

Smoky Mountain Persimmon Bread

3½ cups flour
1 teaspoon salt

Pinch (maybe half a teaspoon) of nutmeg or allspice
2 teaspoons baking soda
2 cups sugar (either brown sugar or refined sugar works fine)
1 cup (2 sticks) melted butter (allow to cool to room temperature after melting)
4 large eggs, lightly whisked
⅔ cup bourbon (a cheap brand is fine)
2 brimming cups of persimmon pulp (fruits should be squishy ripe, and incidentally, pulp freezes well)
1 cup black walnuts (you can substitute 2 cups lightly toasted and chopped pecans or English walnuts)
2 cups dried fruit, such as apricots, raisins, yellow raisins or dates

Preheat oven to 350. Butter a pair of loaf pans or use nonstick pans. Sift flour, salt, spice, baking soda and sugar into a large plastic mixing bowl. Whisk in the butter, eggs, bourbon and persimmon pulp until thoroughly mixed. Add and whisk in nuts and dried fruit. Place batter in pans and slide into preheated oven. Check periodically as bread begins to brown by inserting a toothpick. When the toothpick comes out clean, the bread is ready. Cooking time varies depending on the configuration of pans you use.

Slices of Smoky Mountain persimmon bread. *Tipper Pressley.*

NOTE: Once cooled, wrap to keep moist. The bread will keep several days (but likely be eaten much sooner), and it freezes well. It is rich and somewhat reminiscent of a dark fruitcake.

—Jim Casada

Cocoa Bread with Peaches

1 cup boiling water
½ cup butter, melted
½ cup sorghum syrup
½ cup sugar

45

2 eggs, beaten
2 cups self-rising flour
½ teaspoon baking soda
¼ cup cocoa
I teaspoon cinnamon
Peaches, fresh or canned

Stir together water, butter, sorghum and sugar. Let cool slightly. Stir in eggs. Sift remaining ingredients together; add to water mixture and stir until smooth. Bake in a greased and floured 8-inch square baking pan at 350 degrees for 30 minutes or until done. Top with slices of fresh or canned peaches.

—Tipper Pressley

Molasses Bread

2 cups plain flour
½ teaspoon salt
I teaspoon ginger
2 teaspoons baking powder
¼ teaspoon baking soda
I teaspoon cinnamon
⅓ cup melted butter
I cup molasses
¾ cup buttermilk
I egg

Sift all dry ingredients together. Stir in melted butter and molasses, mixing well. Add milk and egg; mix well. Pour mixture into a greased loaf pan and bake at 350 for 45 to 50 minutes or until done.

TIP: If you don't have buttermilk available, add I tablespoon of lemon juice to I cup of whole milk as a substitute.

—Tipper Pressley

Chapter 4
PORK

THE MAIN MEAT OF APPALACHIA

U p until the middle of the twentieth century, and in some areas well beyond that point, if you lived on a farm or even in a small town with an acre or two of land, raising hogs for meat was pretty much taken for granted. Often, a few extra pigs would also provide a welcome source of "cash money." Lyrics from Loretta Lynn's poignant autobiographical song "Coal Miner's Daughter" are quite suggestive in that regard.

In the summertime we didn't have shoes to wear,
But in the wintertime we'd all get a brand new pair.
From a mail order catalog, money made from selling a hog,
Daddy always managed to get the money somewhere.

Hog-killing time was a seasonal ritual of immense importance. It marked the culmination of many months of hard work with crops and livestock and was the final, vital step in preparation for the ardors of the coming winter. Fittingly, hogs were most commonly butchered a week or two before Thanksgiving, and once lard had been rendered, sausage and cracklings canned, hams launched in the early steps of the smoking or curing process and lesser cuts salted down to provide fatback and streaked meat for the months ahead, country folks could come about as close to rest as they ever did. The menfolk had some spare time for hunting, womenfolk could look with pride on the year's final additions to cannery shelves and everyone feasted on pork. From the magical day in November when many hands

A group of men—(*left to right*) Harrison Caldwell, Emm Anderson and Carl Caldwell—preparing to deal with a huge hog. *Courtesy of Hunter Library, Western Carolina University.*

A group of men at hog-killing time, with a hog hung and cauldrons of scalding water ready. *Courtesy of the National Park Service.*

pitched in for the hard work of killing and processing hogs forward, one key part of life's annual cycle had ended and another one begun. Along with spring's greening-up time, it marked a key moment in how life was lived and what foods were consumed.

Almost without exception, pork was *the* meat in Appalachian daily diet. Chicken was reserved for special occasions (that explains the name frequently applied to it, preacher bird), and beef was a rarity, while fish and game depended on sporting success and/or available time to take to the woods or waters. Pork, by way of sharp contrast, was consumed in some form virtually every day, and more often than not, it made an appearance in two or three meals.

Breakfasts tended to be large and, by today's standards, would be reckoned lavish. Pork offered in some fashion—sausage, bacon, scrapple, head cheese, country ham, liver mush, streaked meat or gravy based on a cut of pork or renderings from the meat—was pretty much standard breakfast fare. With the notable exception of ham, most breakfast meats, at least as the two of us have known them, come from scraps and inferior pieces of pork. Furthermore, aside from venison sausage, we have almost no recollections of other meats for breakfast.

Country Ham and Egg Omelet

2 large eggs
1 tablespoon water
1 pat (tablespoon) butter
1 thin slice country ham, chopped fine
Black pepper to taste

Whisk eggs together with water. Melt butter in a medium-sized nonstick skillet or a well-seasoned cast-iron skillet (or use an omelet pan). Meanwhile, chop slice of country ham into small pieces. When the butter is melted, reduce heat to medium, pour whisked eggs into the pan and dot top with ham bits. Cook until omelet is solid on the bottom and around the edges and then turn it. When omelet is firm, slide the cooked egg-and-pork combination from the skillet onto a plate and serve immediately. No salt is needed because of the saltiness of the ham.

NOTE: This basic omelet can be fancified to suit all sorts of tastes through the addition of ingredients such as cheese, chives, chopped onions, cilantro, parsley and the like.

—Jim Casada

Pork roast with kraut fresh from the oven. *Tipper Pressley.*

Pork Roast with Kraut

Passing along food traditions to the next generation is widely celebrated in Appalachian culture. When I was first married, there was considerable reliance on kitchen knowledge my mother and grandmothers had shared. A pleasant and rewarding surprise came from learning traditional foodways from my new family. My mother-in-law, Miss Cindy, taught me a deliciously easy way to cook an outstanding pork roast with a jar of kraut.

2- to 3-pound pork roast (tenderloin or butt works well)
Salt
Pepper
Flour
Butter, lard or your preferred cooking oil
1 quart homemade kraut (store-bought can also be used)

Season roast and dredge in flour. Heat pan with oil and sear roast on all sides. Transfer roast to a Dutch oven or roasting pan. Pour kraut with liquid over the roast. Cover and cook at 350 degrees until done.

TIP: Potatoes can be added before the roast finishes cooking. This roast goes very well with a cake of cornbread.

—Tipper Pressley

Backbones-and-Ribs

Unless you know a butcher and can get him to custom cut for you, don't count on finding this traditional New Year's staple on grocery shelves. You can find ribs, but invariably, they will have been cut away from the backbone. That's too bad, because the bits of meat where the ribs meet the backbone give credence to the old adage "the closer to the bone, the sweeter the meat." If you obtain only ribs, be sure to get the entire bone, for the end where the rib meets the backbone will soften in cooking and provide tasty marrow to suck or for making bone broth.

Cooking backbones-and-ribs, or whatever cuts of pork you manage to obtain as the closest possible substitute, is the essence of simplicity: trim off excess fat, place in a slow cooker with a bit of water and cook for several hours. With the addition of salt and pepper to taste, you have some simple stuff fit for a king. If you have leftovers, chop up the meat, add your favorite barbecue sauce and you've got the makings of fine barbecue sandwiches.

—Jim Casada

Baked Ham

Ham is often served as the centerpiece of celebratory meals in the mountains of Appalachia. Throughout much of the Appalachian South, an Easter without ham would be as alien as one without dyed eggs for the youngsters. The trick to having a wonderfully tender and moist ham is to avoid overcooking. This recipe is a straightforward, simple approach to baking a ham.

Smoked ham with bone in
2 cups water

Remove thick, rubbery skin from ham. Place in roasting pan fat side up. Pour water around ham. Cover tightly. Bake at 350 degrees for 10 minutes per pound or until heated thoroughly.

TIP: Near the end of the baking process, the cover of the roasting pan can be removed to allow the ham to brown. Be sure to save the ham bone for your next pot of soup beans.

—Tipper Pressley

Glazed Ham Steak

1-inch-thick ham steak
½ cup sorghum syrup
3 tablespoons water
¼ cup orange juice
1 tablespoon brown sugar
½ teaspoon mustard powder
⅛ teaspoon cloves

Place ham in a shallow baking pan. Combine other ingredients and mix well. Pour over ham steak and bake at 375 degrees for 30 minutes, basting occasionally with the liquid in the pan.

TIP: Serve with baked sweet potatoes and biscuits.

—Tipper Pressley

Fatback

Fatback is salt pork and is used often in Appalachian foodways. Although technically, fatback and streaked meat are two different portions of a pig, confusion can reign supreme when you add other descriptions such as streak-o-lean, side meat, salt bacon, pork belly and the like. Throughout this work, the terms fatback *and* streaked meat *are used interchangeably. They are normally purchased in one of two forms—already sliced or in a thick hunk that requires slicing.*

Fry the meat in a cast-iron pan on both sides until done. To prevent curling, cut slits in the edges or use a press to ensure the slices lie flat and cook evenly.

NOTE: Fatback can also be breaded with flour before frying. It goes wonderfully well in a biscuit, with a slice of cornbread or crumbled up over scrambled eggs.

TIP: If the meat is too salty, soak in water for an hour before cooking. Drain and pat dry before frying.

—Jim Casada

Easy Oven Bacon

Oven bacon. *Tipper Pressley.*

While the standard approach to preparing bacon is in the frying pan, it does quite nicely in an oven. Spread bacon on rimmed baking sheet and cook in 400-degree oven until done. Bacon drippings can be saved or poured in a pan as the beginning for gravy.

—Tipper Pressley

Country Ham

Fry ham in a cast-iron skillet, cooking on both sides until done (and to obtain the beginnings of red-eye gravy; see chapter 11).

TIP: To prevent curling, slice edges or use a press to ensure slices lie flat and cook evenly. A smaller cast-iron pan makes an ideal press.

—Tipper Pressley

Streaked Meat Dutch Oven Potatoes

Thoroughly scrub 5 or 6 good-sized baking potatoes and then quarter them. Place in a Dutch oven and sprinkle with black pepper to taste. Cover with strips of fatback and cook at 400 degrees for about an hour. Check while cooking to be sure they aren't overheating. Use a fork to make certain the potatoes are done. You may need to add salt, but do not do this until after the potatoes are cooked. The streaked meat will usually contain enough salt to season them.

—Jim Casada

Streaked Meat and Hominy

Streaked meat works wonders with the somewhat bland taste of hominy. Instead of butter and black pepper—the seasonings most commonly associated with hominy (and, for that matter, hominy grits)—just fry a few thin slices of meat until crispy brown, crumble and sprinkle atop hot hominy. If desired, add a bit of salt to taste (keeping in mind the fact that you are dealing with salt pork) and sprinkle with black pepper.

—Jim Casada

Kale and Sausage Stew

Pork in general, including sausage, has long been an integral part of Appalachian diet and the region's most important meat. This versatile stew—which can be varied with substitute ingredients such as turnip or mustard greens for kale, Italian sausage for traditional mountain pork sausage or about any type of dried bean for cannellini—is wonderfully filling along with being delicious.

I pound kale
I tablespoon olive oil
I pound sausage, shaped into small balls or chunks
I potato
I–2 cloves garlic, chopped
I teaspoon red pepper flakes
I (15-ounce) can cannellini beans, drained and rinsed
3 cups chicken stock
Salt and pepper to taste

Tear kale leaves from the stems, saving the stems. Pile up the leaves and cut into strips with an ulu or knife. Cut the stems into small pieces and set aside. Place oil in a Dutch oven and bring to medium-high heat. Brown the sausage, using a spoon or tongs to turn so it is brown on all sides. Remove the sausage with a slotted spoon and set aside. Add the potato and cook for several minutes, stirring a bit, until the pieces begin to brown. Stir in the kale stems and cook for 3 or 4 minutes. Stir in the garlic, pepper flakes and kale leaves and cook for I additional minute. Return the sausage to the pan and add the drained beans and chicken stock, along with salt and pepper. Adjust the latter two to taste (if the stock is store-bought, it may already have ample salt). Reduce heat and simmer about 10 minutes.

—Jim Casada

Sausage Soup

A hearty meal of soup always seems to lift the spirits, and it's wonderful for dispelling mollygrubs in the depths of winter. That holds doubly true for sausage soup, because it's a stick-to-the-ribs treat that satisfies in tasty fashion and is fit to sustain even those who work incredibly hard.

I pound pork sausage
2 cans beans (kidney, navy or other favorite)
I quart diced or quartered tomatoes
½ cup chopped green pepper
Water as needed to thin soup
I large onion, chopped
I ½ teaspoons garlic powder
½ teaspoon thyme
Salt and pepper to taste
I cup diced potato

Brown sausage in a stock pot. Drain fat. Combine the remaining ingredients—except the potatoes—with the sausage. Simmer for about an hour. Add the potatoes and cook until they are tender. This soup goes well with cornbread.

TIP: Seasonings can be increased, decreased or changed according to individual preferences. For example, a crumbled pod of red pepper in the soup will give it a bit of added heat or "bite."

—Tipper Pressley

Fried Pork Tenderloin

Even folks who were squeamish about the actual process of hog killing and the undeniably odiferous, odious work that followed eagerly anticipated the feast of fresh meat that the day offered. For many with lingering links to a vanishing way of life, the entire event looms large in nostalgic recollection. Of all the appetizing delicacies provided by fresh pork, for most, tenderloin was at the top of the list. Appalachia is full of heartwarming stories of the first mess of fried tenderloin following a day of butchering. Here's a simple, straightforward way to prepare tenderloin, and for most folks in the region, this approach, maybe with slight variations, was what they used.

Salt
Pepper
Flour
Chunks of tenderloin sliced in ½-inch rounds (a thinner or thicker cut may be used)

Mix salt and pepper to taste with the flour. Dredge pork pieces in the flour mixture and fry in hot bacon grease until done. A pan of cathead biscuits and a side of fried apples brings forth the wonderful flavor of the pork in a larger-than-life fashion.

TIP: This recipe works fine with store-bought pork tenderloin, but nothing quite matches the fresh option.

—Tipper Pressley

Chapter 5

PREACHER BIRD

While chicken is today among the less expensive meats found in your local grocery store—though none of them is cheap—there was a time when yard bird appeared on the family table only for special occasions. Chicken was normally served only for holidays, a birthday, Sunday dinner with the preacher in attendance (hence the title of this

Chicken was invariably a featured dish for picnics, church outings or reunions. *Courtesy of Hunter Library, Western Carolina University.*

chapter) or a visit from a family member who had not been seen for some time. The lyrics that state, "We'll kill the old red rooster when she comes," and "We'll all have chicken and dumplings when she comes," are suggestive in that regard, as is the wording of the thankful remembrance written by legendary singer/songwriter/storyteller Tom T. Hall and sung by Bobby Bare and numerous other country musicians, "Chicken every Sunday, Lord, chicken every Sunday."

Anna Lou's Fried Chicken

Every dedicated and skilled kitchen wizard has a few recipes that stand out as being truly special. My mother, Anna Lou Casada, was gifted with a wide array of culinary skills, but when it came to frying chicken, she invariably outdid herself. It was the standard Sunday meat on the family table.

1 (or more) chickens cut into frying portions (legs, thighs, wings and halved breast), skin intact
1 or 2 eggs, whisked
Flour
Salt and pepper to taste
Lard or cooking oil (cast-iron skillets should have between ⅛ and ¼ inch, and I can't imagine using any other utensil to fry chicken)

Drench each piece of chicken in the egg wash and then coat thoroughly with flour (mix salt and pepper in with the flour) before placing in piping hot oil in a large cast-iron pan. It is important that the oil be so hot the chicken sizzles immediately on contact; otherwise, it will soak up too much oil. Reduce heat once pieces begin to brown and continue to cook slowly until thoroughly brown and done.

All of this seems simple and straightforward enough, but it was Mom's final step that made all the difference. Once she had all the chicken fried and placed atop paper towels to drain a bit, she would drain and clean the cast-iron skillet and then put the fried chicken back in it. She next turned the oven on at low heat (200 degrees or maybe a bit less) and put the chicken in it. She normally did this just before heading off to church. When we returned home after church, and once she had readied the rest of the meal, Mom would pop the skillet out of the oven and serve the chicken immediately. Being in the oven seemed to do two things—cook away some of the surplus grease and make the chicken so tender it almost fell from the bones and melted in your mouth.

TIPS:
1. For crustier chicken, do the egg wash/flouring process twice.
2. Use tongs to ever so gently turn the chicken in the pan and transfer it to a serving plate.

—Jim Casada

Baked Fried Chicken

Baked fried chicken. *Tipper Pressley.*

8 chicken pieces
Buttermilk, enough to marinate chicken
2 tablespoons half-and-half
1 egg
1 cup bread crumbs
1 teaspoon garlic salt
¼ teaspoon pepper
Olive oil
3 tablespoons butter, melted

Marinate chicken in buttermilk for several hours. Drain chicken and discard buttermilk. Mix half-and-half with egg and whisk. Mix dry ingredients together and whisk. Dip chicken in the wet mixture and then in the dry one. Place chicken on a baking sheet. Drizzle with olive oil and melted butter. Bake at 450 degrees for 15 minutes and then reduce heat to 400 degrees and continue baking for 35 minutes or until done.

—Tipper Pressley

Baked Whole Chicken

1 onion, quartered or chopped roughly
4 carrots, chopped
2 potatoes, quartered or chopped roughly
2 teaspoons paprika
2 teaspoons garlic powder
1 teaspoon onion powder
1 teaspoon oregano
1 teaspoon thyme
1 teaspoon salt
½ teaspoon pepper
1 whole chicken
1 tablespoon olive oil
½ lemon
1 or 2 rosemary sprigs

Place vegetables on the bottom of a roasting pan or Dutch oven in a single layer. Stir seasonings together. Pat chicken dry and then rub with olive oil. Spread seasonings over the chicken. Place lemon and rosemary in the chicken's body cavity. Cover and cook chicken in a 450-degree oven for 15 minutes and then reduce heat for the remaining cooking time to 350 degrees. After the first 15 minutes, you will need to cook 20 minutes for each pound of chicken. Since this recipe involves a fair amount of prep and cooking time, you will probably want to choose a large baking hen for use. Cover can be removed during the last 20 minutes of cooking to crisp up the skin.

TIP: Leftovers can be used in a variety of ways. The next recipe in this chapter is one example.

—Tipper Pressley

Chicken Stew

Chicken soup is associated with being a bit under the weather for good reason. It's nutritious, tasty, filling and somehow seems just the thing for when, as my Grandpa Joe would have put it, "a body is ailing a bit."

Curiously, I don't remember his wife, Grandma Minnie, ever making chicken soup or indeed soup of any kind, although her stews, laced with meat and vegetables swimming in gravy, were in essence just thickened soups. This recipe is similar to the manner in which she prepared chicken stew. She usually did so when there were a couple of leftover carcasses from baked hens served at holidays (we almost always had hens the family had grown as opposed to store-bought turkey) or when an old hen had been sufficiently derelict in her egg-laying duties to invite consumption. The stew made a great wintertime dish, especially when a heaping platter of cathead biscuits was served as a side.

1 or 2 whole baked hens or a turkey carcass with ample leftover meat scraps
1 large onion, peeled and quartered
4 ribs celery with leaves, chopped
1 large carrot, scrubbed and cut into chunks
2 whole cloves garlic
1 bay leaf
Water to cover

Remove skin from the carcass. Place carcass in a stockpot and surround with onion, celery, carrot, garlic and bay leaf. Cover with water and bring to a boil. Reduce heat and simmer, covered, for two hours. Refrigerate stock until it congeals and remove fat that accumulates on the top. Remove all meat from bones and save.

8 cups stock (add canned chicken broth if needed)
2 cups milk
4 medium potatoes, peeled and diced
3 carrots, peeled and diced
3 ribs celery, diced
1 cup frozen or canned lima beans
2 ounces small-shell pasta
2 cups fresh, chopped spinach
1 cup frozen green peas
Meat from carcass
¼ cup fresh parsley
½ teaspoon dried basil
1 teaspoon fresh black pepper
Salt to taste

1 cup evaporated milk
2 tablespoons flour mixed with 4 tablespoons water
(optional, if you want a thicker stew)

Cook stock, milk, potatoes, carrots and celery for half an hour. Add lima beans, pasta, spinach, peas, meat, parsley, basil and pepper to the soup and cook an additional 20 minutes. Remove from heat, season with salt if necessary and stir in evaporated milk. Return to low heat, stirring often. Do not let stew boil. Thicken with a flour-and-water paste if desired. Makes 12 hearty servings.

TIP: Vegetables other than those mentioned, such as green beans or corn, can be used.

—Jim Casada

Oven Chicken with Gravy

1 cup flour
2 tablespoons garlic powder, divided
1 teaspoon onion powder
1 teaspoon paprika
Salt and pepper to taste
6 bone-in chicken thighs (other cuts may be used)
¼ cup oil
1 onion, chopped
1 teaspoon thyme
2 tablespoons butter
2 cups chicken stock
½ cup milk

Combine flour, 1 tablespoon garlic powder, onion powder, paprika, salt and pepper. Set aside 2 tablespoons. Dredge chicken pieces in flour mixture. Heat oil and brown both sides of chicken in an oven-safe pan; a deep cast-iron pan is ideal. Remove chicken from pan. Add onion to hot pan and stir until tender—about 3 minutes. Add thyme, 1 teaspoon garlic powder and butter, stirring to melt butter. Add reserve flour mixture and cook while stirring for 2 minutes. Add chicken stock slowly and stir well to prevent lumping. Add milk and continue stirring. Season with salt and pepper to taste. Continue cooking until the mixture begins to boil and thicken slightly. At that point, place the chicken pieces back in gravy, cover, put in oven and bake at 400 degrees for an hour.

TIP: Serve over rice or mashed potatoes.

—Tipper Pressley

Chicken and Dumplings

3 pounds of chicken pieces
Water (enough to stew chicken—about 2 quarts)
1 carrot, diced
1 celery stalk, diced
1 onion, diced
¾ teaspoon salt
½ teaspoon pepper
2 cups all-purpose flour
2 teaspoons baking powder
1 teaspoon salt
⅓ cup shortening or lard

Combine the first seven ingredients in a large saucepot. Bring to a boil and simmer until chicken is tender. Remove chicken from broth. After it has cooled, debone and chop or shred. Vegetables can be discarded or left in the broth. Skim fat from broth, if desired. Reserve ⅔ cup of broth for making dumplings. Return chicken to the pot.

Chicken and dumplings ready for a fine supper. *Tipper Pressley.*

Combine flour, baking powder and 1 teaspoon of salt. Cut shortening in with pastry cutter or fork until crumbly. Add reserved broth and stir with fork. Turn dough out onto a floured surface and knead lightly. Roll dough out to ⅛-inch thickness and cut into 2-inch squares to make your dumplings.

Bring broth back to a boil and drop dumplings in it one at a time. Reduce heat, cover and simmer for 30 minutes or until done.

—Tipper Pressley

Chicken Casserole

2 cups cooked shredded chicken
3 cups cooked broccoli
½ cup mayonnaise
1 teaspoon lemon juice
¼ teaspoon paprika
1 can cream of mushroom soup
1 can cream of chicken soup
1 cup grated cheddar cheese
1 stick butter, melted
2 cups seasoned bread crumbs or stuffing mix

Combine all ingredients except butter and bread crumbs and pour in 9" × 13" pan. Mix melted butter with bread crumbs and sprinkle on top. Bake at 350 degrees for 25 minutes.

—Tipper Pressley

Chapter 6
BEEF

For the people of rural Appalachia in yesteryear, beef did not figure prominently in daily diet. While most families owned one or two milk cows and while milk, butter, cheese and buttermilk were of considerable importance, beef seldom appeared on the menu. A family may even have owned other cattle, but if they were so blessed, the livestock were used as draft animals to plow, pull sleds, help with logging, assist in road building and the like. Moreover, pork was far easier to preserve

A hefty slice of meat loaf makes mighty fine eating. *Tipper Pressley.*

than beef, not to mention that hogs required appreciably less care, were hardier and were capable of "running wild" while fattening themselves up during the fall. Still, beef began to creep into Appalachian menus with increasing frequency during and after the Depression, and inclusion of a selection of recipes featuring the meat (mostly the cheaper cuts or in ground form) seems appropriate. Beef is, of course, far more prominent in today's Appalachian cooking.

Vegetable Beef Soup

For this recipe, you'll be taking whatever leftover vegetables you might have in the refrigerator (corn, field peas, limas, green beans or the like) and combining them with other basic vegetables after they have cooked.

1 onion, chopped
Several celery stalks, chopped
4 to 6 carrots, chopped
2 potatoes, chopped in small pieces or diced
Beef broth, enough to cover the vegetables
2 or 3 turnips, sliced (optional)
2 cups ground beef or venison (more if you like a meaty soup)
Olive oil
Leftover vegetables (already cooked), if you have any available
Salt and pepper to taste

Begin by chopping up the onion, celery, carrots and potatoes; cook them in beef broth (you can buy canned broth, use the paste that mixes with water or buy bones to make your own) until almost tender. At that point, if you like them (I do), add turnips. They don't take nearly as long to cook as the other veggies, so they should be introduced relatively late in the cooking process. Meanwhile, brown ground beef (or venison, which works equally well in this recipe) in a bit of olive oil. When it is completely browned, add it and the leftover vegetables to the cooked ones. Add additional broth if needed to get soup at the liquid-to-ingredients ratio you want. Salt and pepper to taste and allow to simmer slowly for an hour or so in order for the flavors to blend. Served with a big piece of cornbread, this makes a fine meal.

TIP: You can take pretty much the same approach with the carcass of a baked wild turkey or the dark meat of a wild turkey that has been cooked until it comes away from the bones. In this case, be sure to use the turkey stock.

—Jim Casada

Simple Oven Stew

¼ cup flour
½ teaspoon salt
¼ teaspoon black pepper
2 pounds stew meat, cut into 1-inch cubes
3–4 tablespoons canola oil
4–5 medium potatoes, peeled and cut into chunks
4–5 large carrots, cut into chunks
2 ribs celery, cut into chunks
1 large onion, cut into slices
1 package onion soup mix
3 cups water

Mix flour, salt and pepper in a paper bag. Add meat cubes and shake well. Brown meat in oil and place in a large casserole. Add potatoes, carrots, celery, onion, onion soup mix and water. Cover and cook at 325 degrees for 2 hours or until meat and vegetables are tender.

—Jim Casada

Shepherd's Pie

1 pound ground beef
1 onion, finely chopped
1 cup chopped mushrooms (optional)
1 large can tomato sauce
Salt and pepper to taste

2 cans green beans or 1 quart of home-canned ones, drained
1 pound cooked mashed potatoes (the real thing—a plague on the paltry
powdered substitutes. Leftover mashed potatoes work just fine.)
1 cup grated cheddar cheese

Brown ground beef with onions and mushrooms. Drain, if necessary. Add tomato sauce, salt and pepper to meat mixture.

In a deep baking dish, layer green beans, ground beef and tomato sauce mixture; cover with mashed potatoes and sprinkle grated cheese on top. Bake at 350 degrees for about 30 minutes or until heated through.

TIP: As is the case more often than not, especially in the ground form, beef and venison are pretty much interchangeable in this and most other beef recipes in this book—and, for that matter, in general.

—Jim Casada

Country-Style Steak

⅓ cup flour
Salt and pepper to taste
1 pound steak, cubed
2 tablespoons olive oil
1 medium onion
1 (4-ounce) jar whole mushrooms
1 to 1½ cups water

Mix flour, salt and pepper. Dredge steak in flour and brown quickly in oil. Place in an 8" × 11" casserole dish. Slice onion and cook in a saucepan until tender. Place on top of steak along with drained mushrooms. Add two tablespoons of the remaining flour to pan drippings. Stir until brown, add 1 to 1½ cups of water and cook until thick. Pour over steaks. Bake covered in a 350-degree oven for an hour or until tender.

—Jim Casada

Oven Meatballs

2 pounds ground beef
1 cup quick or regular oats (not instant)
1 cup soft bread crumbs
½ cup milk
1 teaspoon salt
Flour
1 envelope dry onion soup mix
1 ½ cups water

Mix ground beef, oats, bread crumbs, milk and salt; roll into 2-inch balls. Roll meatballs in flour and place in a casserole dish. Pour 1 envelope dry onion soup mix and 1 ½ cups water over meatballs. Bake at 350 degrees for an hour.

—Jim Casada

Tipper's Favorite Meatloaf

1 pound hamburger meat
1 slice of bread, crumbled
1 onion, chopped
1 egg
1 teaspoon salt
1 teaspoon pepper
¼ (8-ounce) can tomato sauce
1 ½ tablespoons vinegar
¾ (8-ounce) can tomato sauce
1 ½ tablespoons brown sugar
1 tablespoon Worcestershire sauce
1 teaspoon mustard

Mix the first seven ingredients together and put in a loaf pan. I line my pan with foil for easier cleanup. Mix the rest of the ingredients together and pour over meatloaf. Take a spatula or case knife and help the liquid seep down into the cracks along the side; give the middle a poke or two, as well. Bake at 375 degrees for 1 hour and 15 minutes. Toward the end of the cooking, pour off grease that has ponded in the loaf pan and put the pan back into the oven to finish cooking. This may not be necessary—it depends on the fat content of the meat you use.

TIP: This recipe is easily doubled. I almost always double it so that we have leftovers to enjoy for dinner during the week.

—Tipper Pressley

Hamburger and Beans

1 pound ground beef
½ cup diced onion
1 can baked beans
1 tablespoon sugar (or less to taste)

Brown ground beef and onions; drain fat. Add beans and sugar; stir to combine. Heat through. Serve on buns or over rice.

TIP: Leftover homemade baked beans may also be used.

—Tipper Pressley

Tender Cubed Steak

Cubed steak
Flour
Seasonings
Olive oil (or your preference)
Chicken stock

Dredge cubed steak in flour seasoned to your taste. I like to use salt, pepper and garlic powder. Heat olive oil, or whatever oil you prefer, in a frying pan and bring to medium heat. Place floured, seasoned cubed steak in hot pan and brown on each side, but don't worry about cooking through. Once both sides are browned, place cubed steak in a slow cooker.

Cubed steak ready for flouring and frying. *Tipper Pressley.*

Add a tablespoon or two of flour to the frying pan like you were going to make gravy from the drippings. Cook and stir flour for a few minutes and then pour in chicken stock. Continue to cook and stir while gently scraping the cooked pieces off the bottom of the pan.

After a few minutes of cooking, pour chicken stock over cubed steak in the slow cooker. I aim to have enough chicken stock to almost cover the steak. Then cook on low for several hours or until done. The meat turns out super tender, and the broth makes gravy that is perfect for putting over mashed potatoes or rice.

TIP: Use flour leftover from dredging to make gravy.

—Tipper Pressley

Cabbage Patch Stew

Stew
1 pound ground beef
2 medium onions, thinly sliced
1 ½ cups cabbage, coarsely chopped
3 or 4 celery stalks, with leaves
1 (16-ounce) can stewed tomatoes
1 (15-ounce) can kidney beans
1 cup water
1 teaspoon salt
¼ teaspoon pepper
1 to 2 teaspoons chili powder

Dumplings
2 cups biscuit baking mix
⅔ cup milk
Paprika (optional)

A bowl of cabbage patch stew hot from the pot. *Tipper Pressley.*

Cook and stir ground beef in Dutch oven until brown; drain. Add onions, cabbage and celery; cook and stir until vegetables are light brown (about 10 minutes). Stir in tomatoes, kidney beans with liquid, water, salt, pepper and chili powder. Heat to boiling and then reduce heat.

To make dumplings for the stew, mix baking mix with milk until soft dough forms. Drop by spoonfuls onto the boiling stew. Cook uncovered over low heat for 10 minutes. Cover and cook for an additional 10 minutes. Sprinkle dumplings with paprika, if desired.

TIP: This stew is really good with crackers or cornbread, if you want to skip the dumplings.

—Tipper Pressley

Chapter 7
MEAT FROM NATURE'S LARDER

In yesteryear, especially in the leanest of times, hardy Appalachian folks gladly supplemented the domestic meat portion of their diet with wild game and fish. Prior to the sad demise of that giant of eastern forests, the American chestnut, squirrels were incredibly abundant. Other small game, notably rabbits and birds (to the uninitiated, *birds* referred to quail, while grouse were variously known as pottiges or pheasants), was plentiful in many areas. Even songbirds were utilized. Jim's Grandpa Joe Casada loved to ruminate on trapping snowbirds (juncos) by the dozens and eating them in bird pies. In more remote regions, prior to being all but extirpated, deer and wild turkeys provided welcome provender, and one of the interesting aspects of modern conservation efforts is the manner in which those two species have made major comebacks and thus have once more become prominent on many an Appalachian table.

Anna Lou's Squirrel

2 squirrels, dressed
Water to cover meat
1 teaspoon baking soda
2 tablespoons butter

A wee youngster holds a brace of cottontails, obviously killed or trapped by a family member, that are destined for the family table. *Courtesy of Hunter Library, Western Carolina University.*

Place squirrels in large saucepan. Cover with cold water, add baking soda and heat to boiling. Remove from heat and rinse squirrels well under cold, running water, rubbing to remove soda. Return to pan and cover with fresh water. Bring to a boil; reduce heat and simmer until tender. Place squirrels in a baking dish, dot with butter and bake at 350 degrees until browned and crusty (usually 10 to 15 minutes).

This was my Mom's (her name was Anna Lou) favorite way to cook squirrel. You can prepare rabbit in the same fashion.

—Jim Casada

Rabbit with Lima Beans

2 rabbits, dressed and cut into pieces
Flour, salt and pepper
¼ pound bacon
2 cups dried lima beans, looked and then soaked overnight
1 onion, chopped
2 celery ribs, chopped
2 carrots, chopped
2 cups boiling hot water
1 tablespoon sugar
1 cup sliced okra
3 potatoes, diced
2 cups frozen corn
2 (16-ounce) cans stewed tomatoes
1 bay leaf
Dash thyme and parsley
½ teaspoon crushed red pepper (optional)

Dredge rabbit pieces in flour, salt and pepper mixture. In Dutch oven, fry bacon and remove. Brown rabbit in bacon drippings, then return bacon and add lima beans, onion, celery and carrots, covering with boiling water. Simmer for two hours, adding water if necessary. The meat can be removed from the bones at this point, if you wish. Add remaining ingredients and simmer for an hour longer or until rabbit and vegetables are tender. If desired, thicken with flour-and-water paste and adjust seasonings. Serves 6 to 8 and is a good way to stretch out a couple of rabbits.

TIP: This recipe works equally well with squirrels.

—Jim Casada

Fried Quail

Except for hunting preserves and some quite special (and costly) situations involving intensive management, quail belong to a world we have lost. Yet they were once a special item in Appalachian diet, and it is still possible to hunt the birds great outdoor writer Havilah Babcock once described as "five ounces of feathered dynamite" in release situations. The culinary aftermath of such outings can be pure delight, thanks to recipes such as this one.

1 cup red wine
1 cup olive oil
1 tablespoon minced garlic
16 dressed quail
3 cups self-rising flour
¼ cup seasoned salt
Vegetable oil for deep frying

Mix the wine, olive oil and garlic. Add the quail and marinate, refrigerated, for 4 to 6 hours. Combine the flour and seasoned salt. Drain the quail and coat in the flour/salt mixture. Deep fry in 350-degree oil for 15 to 20 minutes. Serve immediately. Makes 8 servings.

TIP: The quantities in recipe can be halved, and if you like a bit of "bite," add some black pepper or red pepper flakes to the flour and salt.

—Jim Casada

Apple Quail

¼ cup flour
½ teaspoon salt, or to taste
⅛ teaspoon paprika
6 dressed quail
2 tablespoons butter
¼ cup sweet onion, chopped
1 tablespoon fresh parsley, chopped
¼ teaspoon dried thyme
1 cup apple juice

Mix flour, salt and paprika; lightly flour quail pieces. Melt butter in heavy frying pan and brown quail. Push quail to one side of the pan. Add onion and sauté until tender (add 1 tablespoon of additional butter if needed). Add parsley, thyme and apple juice. Stir to mix well and spoon juice over quail while bringing all to a boil. Then reduce heat, cover and simmer until quail are tender (about an hour). Serve quail on a bed of rice or grits with sautéed apples on the side.

—Jim Casada

Wild Turkey Tenders

1 egg
1 tablespoon water
1 pound wild turkey breast, cut into strips (cut across the grain)
1 cup all-purpose flour
½ cup canola oil
Salt and black pepper to taste

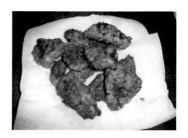

Fried turkey tenders just out of the skillet drain prior to being served. *Jim Casada.*

Beat egg with water. Dredge turkey strips in flour, dip in egg mixture and then dredge again in flour. Fry in canola oil in a cast-iron skillet until brown and tender. Serve immediately.

TIP: If the turkey is not tender (and an old gobbler likely won't be), pound with a meat hammer before frying or else cover and steam a few minutes after you have browned the strips. They will not be as crisp with the latter approach.

—Jim Casada

Mustard-Fried Venison Steak

1 pound venison steak, cubed
½ cup prepared mustard, such as French's
⅔ cup all-purpose flour
1 teaspoon salt
6 tablespoons canola oil

Brush each piece of cubed steak on both sides with mustard. Place flour and salt in a bag and then shake to mix. Add half of steak to bag and shake well to coat thoroughly. Repeat. Heat oil in a nonstick pan or well-seasoned cast-iron skillet and add floured steak. Cook until golden brown, turning only once. Do not overcook—meat should be pink in the middle when removed from the pan. Serve immediately. Makes 3 to 4 servings.

NOTE: Quantities can be doubled (or more), and steak cut into bite-size bits make a dandy hors d'oeuvre.

—Jim Casada

Venison Hot Dog/Burger/Sloppy Joe Chili

1 pound ground venison
⅓ cup chopped onion
1 package Sauer's Chili Seasoning (or use your own)

⅓ cup water
1 (8-ounce) can tomato paste

Brown venison and onion. Add seasoning package or your own personal choices, water and tomato sauce. Simmer 10 to 15 minutes until thick. Serve with hot dogs or burgers or atop a bun as a Sloppy Joe.

—Jim Casada

Venison Noodle Soup

4 cups beef broth
½ pound egg noodles or spaghetti
½ pound ground venison
¼–½ cup olive oil
2 ribs celery, chopped
1 small onion, chopped
2 tablespoons butter or margarine
Garlic salt to taste
Salt and pepper to taste
Chives
Parmesan cheese

Heat broth to boiling and add noodles. In a separate pan, brown venison in olive oil. Sauté celery and onion in butter. When noodles are done, add cooked venison, celery and onion to soup pot. Add garlic salt, salt and pepper to taste. Simmer for 10–15 minutes. Garnish with fresh chives and Parmesan cheese.

TIP: If you have leftover venison burgers, they can be chopped up and used in the soup.

—Jim Casada

Quick Venison Chili

1–2 pounds ground or chopped venison
1 large onion, chopped
1 (14-ounce) can diced tomatoes
1 (16-ounce) can beans (kidney or pinto), drained and rinsed
1 (6-ounce) can tomato paste
1 cup water
1 package chili seasoning
Salt and pepper to taste
Grated cheese
Chives
Crackers

Brown venison and onion. Add tomatoes, drained and rinsed beans, tomato paste, water and seasonings. Simmer 45 minutes or longer for flavors to blend. Serve hot, topped with grated cheese and chives and accompanied by crackers.

—Jim Casada

Deer Roast

Deer ham (roast)
1 stick butter
1 tablespoon minced garlic
Salt
Pepper
Creole seasoning mix (such as Old Bay Seasoning)
Oregano
Bacon slices, enough to cover roast
Toothpicks
Honey
Apple cider vinegar

Place deer ham in a roasting pan or other baking dish. Pour ½ inch of water around the ham. Add butter and garlic into a small pan and cook

A deer roast in a Dutch oven ready to be slow cooked to tender perfection. *Tipper Pressley.*

until butter is melted. Pour mixture over deer ham. Season ham with salt, pepper, Old Bay and oregano to taste. Cover ham with bacon. Toothpicks can be used to secure the bacon strips and keep them from curling up as they cook. Drizzle with honey and a dash of apple cider vinegar. Cover deer ham and bake at 220 degrees for 9 hours or until done. Since the cooking temperature is so low, cooking overnight works wonderfully.

—Tipper Pressley

Grilled Deer Loin

Marinade
Makes enough for half a large tenderloin or a whole small loin.

1 ½ cups olive oil
1 cup Worcestershire sauce
1 ½ teaspoons salt
1 ½ teaspoons black pepper
½ teaspoon garlic powder

½ teaspoon oregano
1 heaping tablespoon honey

Mix well; marinate meat at least 5–6 hours. Cook to your desired doneness, basting loin throughout grilling process with marinade. Discard any leftover marinade.

—Tipper Pressley

Venison Cheeseburger Pie

1 pound ground venison
½ cup evaporated milk
½ cup ketchup
⅓ cup dry bread crumbs
¼ cup chopped onion
½ teaspoon dried oregano or two teaspoons fresh oregano
Salt and pepper to taste
1 (8-inch) prepared pie shell
1 cup sharp cheddar cheese, shredded
1 teaspoon Worcestershire sauce

Combine venison, milk, ketchup, bread crumbs, onion and oregano. Season to taste with salt and pepper. Prepare pastry to line an 8-inch pie plate (use a prepared shell or make your own). Fill with venison mixture. Bake at 350 degrees for 35 to 40 minutes. Toss cheese with Worcestershire sauce; sprinkle atop pie. Bake 10 minutes more. Let stand 10 minutes before slicing and serving.

—Jim Casada

Carolina Doves

½ cup flour
Salt and pepper to taste

16 dove breasts
2 tablespoons butter or margarine
2 tablespoons canola oil

Place flour, salt and pepper in a bag. Shake doves in bag to coat well. Heat butter and oil to medium hot and brown the birds quickly on all sides. Add enough water to cover halfway up on doves. Cover the pan and simmer for 60 to 90 minutes or until doves are tender. Remove doves and thicken the gravy with a flour-and-water paste (two tablespoons flour and two tablespoons water). Serve with rice, biscuits and a green salad or fresh fruit.

—Jim Casada

Chapter 8
FISH

T raditionally, fishing formed a welcome break from the ardors of daily labor in the Appalachians, but it also served the dual purpose of offering some welcome variety to the ordinary diet on the table. One indication that fishing wasn't strictly for sport is provided by the popularity of approaches such as trot lines, limb lines, throw lines, jug fishing, fish traps and even the use of infusions such as juice from walnut hulls to stun fish and bring them to the surface. All were fine ways to get a large catch with minimal effort, and in these approaches, the sport of hook-and-line didn't take primacy of place.

Mountain trout in the process of being dressed for the table. *Tipper Pressley.*

Of course, even with a trusty cane pole rig or maybe store-bought outfits, what was caught went straight to a stringer and from there to the family table. The region offers a wide variety of tasty fish—trout, largemouth and smallmouth bass, bream, crappie, catfish and more. A favorite saying from Jim's mother pretty well sums up matters. Modern-day sport fishermen may talk about "catch and release." In her view, the only proper or sensible approach involved "release to grease." The recipes that follow involve not only frying but also other methods of preparing various fish found in southern Appalachia. Seafood was occasionally utilized, but that is in large measure a modern-day development as opposed to being a traditional part of diet. After all, the Appalachians were an appreciable distance from the ocean, and preservation of fish, other than in salted or canned form, was pretty much a nonstarter.

Pan-Fried Trout

2–3 small trout per person (6–8 inches length is ideal—they are tastier than larger ones)
Stone-ground cornmeal
Salt and pepper
Bacon grease, lard or vegetable oil

Clean the fish and leave damp so they will hold plenty of cornmeal. Put your cornmeal in a bag; add the trout, along with salt and pepper; and shake thoroughly, making sure the body cavity gets coated. Place the trout in a large frying pan holding piping hot grease. Cook, turning only once, until golden brown. You can help the process along by using a spatula to splash grease into the open body cavity. Place cooked fish atop paper towels, pat gently to remove any excess grease and dig in.

NOTE: Quite small trout, 8 inches or smaller, in situations where it is legal to keep them, can be fried sufficiently crisp to eat bones, fins and all.

—Jim Casada

Robert Scoville frying trout streamside in Pisgah National Forest. *Jim Casada.*

Simple Catfish Fillets

1 cup lemon juice
2 pounds catfish fillets
Fish seasoning (your favorite)

Pour the lemon juice into a bowl. Dip fillets in juice and then sprinkle generously with seasoning. Cook on a grill pan or in an oiled skillet for 10 minutes per inch of thickness or until the fish flakes readily.

—Jim Casada

Crappie Delight

2 pounds crappie fillets
¼ cup lemon juice

2 eggs, beaten
¼ cup milk
1 teaspoon salt
1 cup all-purpose flour
Oil for frying
½ cup grated cheddar cheese

Cut fillets into serving-size portions and arrange in a baking dish. Pour lemon juice over fillets and let stand for 6 to 8 minutes, turning once. Combine eggs, milk and salt in a bowl. Roll the fillets in the flour and then dip into the egg mixture. Heat oil in a large skillet and fry fish until brown on one side, then turn. Sprinkle cheese on the cooked side. It will melt as the fish cooks. Serve immediately when done.

—Jim Casada

Catfish Stew

6–7 pounds catfish fillets
5 pounds potatoes
3 pounds onions, diced
1 ½ pounds lean hog jowl or side meat, diced
1 (27-ounce) can diced tomatoes
3 (14-ounce) cans stewed tomatoes
1 (46-ounce) can tomato juice
¼ cup Worcestershire sauce
Salt, black pepper and red pepper to taste

Combine the catfish and enough water to cover the fillets in a soup pot. Bring to a boil and then simmer until the fish flakes easily. Drain and reserve the cooking liquid. Pick through the fish to remove any bones. Refrigerate the fish.

Peel the potatoes or leave peels on, if you prefer. Cut into ½-inch cubes. Add to the pot of fish stock. In a separate saucepot, combine the onions with water to cover them, bring to a boil, cook until tender and add to the soup pot. Fry the hog jowl until crisp. Drain the oil produced by frying the pork and add the meat to the stock pot. Add the fish to the pot along with the diced tomatoes. Cut the stewed tomatoes in small pieces and add them to the pot, as well. Add the tomato juice as needed to prevent the mixture cooking down too much. When potatoes and onions are tender, add the Worcestershire sauce and any remaining tomato juice. Simmer for 2 to 3 hours, stirring occasionally.

Serves 15 and is ideal for a family gathering or community cookout or as a meal for a bunch of buddies gathered in a hunt camp during deer season. You can cut the amount of ingredients for a smaller amount of stew, if desired.

—Jim Casada

Salt and Pepper Catfish

6 cups cornmeal
Salt and black pepper to taste
2 pounds catfish fillets, cut into 1-inch strips
Peanut oil for deep frying

Mix cornmeal with salt and black pepper and toss catfish strips, enough for a fryer full at a time, in a plastic or paper bag. Heat oil to 375 degrees in a deep fryer. Cook the nuggets, a dozen or so at a time, until they are golden brown and begin to float to the top. Drain atop paper towels. This is a recipe that makes 10 to 12 servings, but it can be halved or quartered.

—Jim Casada

Honey Pecan Mountain Trout

½ cup all-purpose flour
Salt and pepper to taste
½ cup finely chopped pecans
2 pounds trout fillets (fillet large trout or split small fish down the middle and remove as many bones as possible—leave the skin in place)

Netting a fine trout at Lake Logan. *Courtesy of Hunter Library, Western Carolina University.*

1 egg, beaten
Butter, softened
Honey

Preheat a grill, broiler or grill pan. Combine the flour, salt and pepper. Spread the pecans on a clean plate or a sheet of waxed paper. Dip the fish in the flour mixture and shake gently to remove the excess. Brush with the egg and then press the fish into the pecans. Dot with butter and drizzle with a little honey. Grill, skin side down first, until partially cooked, then carefully turn and cook through.

—Jim Casada

Trout Baked in Foil

While I'd argue, perhaps with some vehemence, that nothing quite matches fresh-caught trout fried over an open fire in a backcountry campsite, perhaps with a side dish of ramps and branch lettuce or fried potatoes and onions, you can skip the grease and use foil for the cooking process. This works on an open fire if you know what you are doing with coals, on a backyard grill or in the kitchen oven.

1 large or 2 small trout per person
Butter
Lemon, lemon seasoning or herb seasoning

Place each whole, dressed trout in its own container of tinfoil, folding carefully so everything stays inside. Line the body cavity with a couple pats of butter, insert thin slices of lemon or dust with whatever combination of herbs appeals to you (dried parsley, perhaps with just a touch of red pepper flakes, is particularly good). Cook until the flesh easily flakes from the bones, and be aware of the fact this won't take long.

—Jim Casada

Oyster Stew

Although the dish has saltwater origins, many mountain families have long enjoyed a tradition of serving oyster stew on Christmas Eve, and local stores would have the tasty bivalves then but at no other time. This recipe has been handed down through generations in my husband's family.

Fresh oysters
Milk
Butter
Pepper
Salt

Heat milk and butter until hot but not boiling. Add oysters, a heavy sprinkling of pepper and salt to taste. Continue to heat, stirring frequently, until the oysters are cooked through.

TIP: Leftovers can be refrigerated and reheated.

—Tipper Pressley

Chapter 9

YOU'VE GOT TO HAVE GRAVY

G ravy holds a rarified, almost revered place in Appalachian diet. To offer a contextual example from the past, the mere thought of starting out a day without gravy for breakfast with a large-scale logging outfit, at a Civilian Conservation Corps outpost or in a remote backcountry hunting or fishing camp would have been sheer culinary sacrilege. Indeed, the often-used term *sawmill gravy* has its origins in the kitchens that served logging camps. Similarly, no offering of country ham without a side of red-eye gravy would pass muster. Beyond that, on a practical level, gravy has always been an ideal way to impart meat flavor while making a little meat go a long way. Some type of meat figured in the flavor picture, but the primary ingredients were flour, milk (or maybe water) and grease. All were readily available and far less expensive than even the most common cuts of meat.

Gravy was also a most satisfying and frugal way to use the byproduct of any fried meat. It did so in a manner that was filling, cost little and eminently met the oft-heard Appalachian adage of "waste not, want not." When it came to hearty eating, gravy was a finishing touch, a blessing of tasty goodness that rendered the ordinary extraordinary or brought taste-tempting moistness to dry bread or tough meat. One measure of the importance of gravy is that a cook's ability to make it "just right" was considered a key or defining characteristic of overall kitchen ability. To say that a cook made "mighty fine gravy" was to tender a compliment of the highest order.

A mountain farmer readies a field with a walking plow pulled by a pair of horses. *Courtesy of Hunter Library, Western Carolina University.*

Hamburger Gravy

Many Appalachian families a few generations back were more likely to enjoy the flavor of beef in gravy than any other way. A half pound or so of the least expensive ground beef available (i.e., with the highest fat content) could be stretched a long way when made into gravy and served atop biscuits or crumbled cornbread. It was considered a real treat in my youth, possibly because it was served infrequently or thanks to being a change from the far more common offerings of pork.

½ pound ground beef with 25–30 percent fat content
½ cup (or more) all-purpose flour
I cup milk
Salt and pepper to taste

Fry the burger and then drain the grease and set the meat aside. Using the hot grease as your base, make a roux by gradually adding and browning flour. Then pour in milk a bit at a time, stirring constantly as the gravy thickens. When you approach the desired consistency for the gravy, sprinkle in salt and pepper along with adding the reserved burger. Using milk as your thinning agent, reheat until the meat gravy is just right for serving. You can control the thickness of the gravy by how much flour and milk you use, and if the gravy is relatively thin, a little burger goes a long way—and still keeps the taste of beef even though the mixture is mostly milk and flour.

—Jim Casada

Giblet Gravy

While there's nothing wrong with enjoying dressing or a slice of turkey in an unadorned state, why settle for pedestrian fare when both really cry out for a lavish ladle of giblet gravy spooned over them? I'll leave the gravy-making details to your individual tastes, but I do have a suggestion that will make gravy prepared for use with chicken or turkey meatier (and better). For example, the next time you are fortunate enough to kill a wild turkey, save not only the giblets (heart, liver and gizzard) but also all of the dark meat (legs, thighs, wings and medallions on the back). Obviously, you can do the same thing with a store-bought bird, but make sure the giblets are a part of your purchase.

Place the dark meat in a large stockpot and keep it simmering for at least a couple of hours. The dark meat of a wild turkey will never get really tender, but it will reach a point where you can readily remove it from the bones. Do so and keep the stock, as well. Chopped into small pieces and frozen with the giblets (add them in the final half hour of simmering), you have the makings of giblet gravy richly laced with nutritious bits of turkey. Combine it with some of the stock you saved, and you can produce an abundance of gravy and have the good feeling associated with fully utilizing your wild bird or getting the essence of goodness from a domestic one.

TIP: Whenever you bake a store-bought turkey, be sure to save all the juices produced. Since more often than not, such birds have had liquid added through an infusion process, there's usually plenty of juice. Freeze any you don't use at the time. It will come in handy as stock for soups, stews or maybe preparation of a wild bird.

—Jim Casada

Tomato Gravy

2 tablespoons all-purpose flour
2 tablespoons bacon drippings
Dash sugar
2 cups peeled and chopped tomatoes
Water or milk
Salt and pepper to taste

Add flour to hot bacon drippings and cook over medium heat for 1 to 2 minutes or until flour is browned while stirring steadily. Season to taste with salt and pepper as the mixture cooks. Stir in tomatoes and add dash of sugar. Cover and cook over low heat until mixture thickens. Depending on how juicy the tomatoes are, you may need to add milk or water to thin the gravy to the desired consistency. This recipe is a favorite summer breakfast item in many parts of the Appalachians.

TIP: Canned tomatoes may also be used. A variation is to sauté diced onion in the bacon drippings before adding the tomatoes.

—Tipper Pressley

Gravy and Tomatoes

This is a great way to enjoy surplus ground beef or venison. Just brown whatever amount of meat you have, perhaps that leftover from grilling burgers or making a meatloaf, and then add milk and flour, stirring steadily, to make a milk/meat gravy. If the meat is quite lean, as will certainly be the case with venison, you will need to add a bit of cooking oil (or here's another good use for the grease left over from frying streaked meat). Cook to desired thickness and pour over juicy slices of tomato. You can make an open-faced sandwich if you desire, but just the venison gravy and maters make mighty fine fixin's.

—Jim Casada

Chocolate Gravy

Chocolate gravy is a traditional Appalachian breakfast item. My mother said her family often had it when she was a girl when there was no meat to fry for regular gravy. Since it was sweet, the children felt like it was a special treat.

Chocolate gravy. *Tipper Pressley.*

3 tablespoons flour
4 tablespoons sugar
3 tablespoons cocoa
2 cups water

Place flour in cast-iron pan on medium heat; add sugar and cocoa and mix well. Gradually add water to mixture, stirring constantly like you would for any other type of gravy. Serve over warm biscuits.

—Tipper Pressley

Cornmeal Gravy

About 3 or 4 tablespoons bacon, fatback or hog jowl grease
½ cup cornmeal
Milk
Salt and pepper to taste

Brown cornmeal in hot fat; add other ingredients and stir until thickened. You've probably noticed this is not an exact recipe. I've found making gravy to be one of those things you have to do over

Working a rocky field with a walking plow and an ox. *Courtesy of National Park Service.*

and over until you figure out the method that works best for you. I add cornmeal or flour by the spoonful until I get enough in the pan to soak up all the grease as it browns. Then I add milk to my thickness preference. I like my gravy thin, so I use more milk than most folks. As the gravy cooks, you can add additional milk or water to thin it out if it gets too thick on you.

—Tipper Pressley

Sausage/Bacon/Fatback Gravy

Fried sausage, bacon or fatback (quantity can vary widely,
but you need enough to produce adequate drippings for gravy)
3 tablespoons flour
Salt and pepper (black or red) to taste
1½ cups milk (a bit more may be needed)

After frying meat, add 2 to 3 tablespoons of flour to drippings and allow to cook for 2 to 3 minutes while stirring constantly. Salt, pepper and other seasoning can be added at this point. As you stir, try to raise any little bits of meat that have cooked onto the pan. Doing so will ensure a very flavorful gravy. Slowly add milk to pan, stirring constantly. About 1½ cups of milk is usually needed, but of course, that will be adjusted according to the amount of grease you have. I like my gravy on the thin side, so after it cooks about 5 minutes, if I need to adjust the thickness, I add a little more milk to thin it out. Serve over warm biscuits.

TIP: Gravy is also delicious over toast and cornbread.

—Tipper Pressley

Red-Eye Gravy

Country ham
Coffee

This is the easiest gravy to make! Fry country ham in a cast-iron pan. Remove from pan once browned on both sides. Pour hot coffee into the hot drippings and stir while scraping bottom of pan. Allow to simmer for a few minutes, and it's ready to eat. Pour over hot biscuits and enjoy!

TIP: Some folks who don't particularly like coffee substitute water in the gravy-making process.

—Tipper Pressley

Chapter 10

SPRING VEGETABLES

T he season's first meal featuring any vegetable or fruit is invariably welcomed with gustatory warmth, but this is particularly true of spring. After months of relying on canned, dried or frozen foods, long-term keepers such as winter squash or items from grocery store shelves that never achieve the same standards of deliciousness as vegetables fresh from the garden, spring brings pure culinary joy. The recipes that follow offer a savory sampling of eats linked to earth's annual reawakening as it takes place in the Appalachians.

Plowing a rocky field with a walking plow pulled by a steer. *Courtesy of the National Park Service.*

New Potatoes

The first new potatoes of the year are looked forward to from the moment seed potatoes are carefully cut and planted in late winter. Southern Appalachian folks will often rush the enjoyment of this dietary staple by grabbling (gently removing small potatoes without pulling up the entire plant), while allowing other tubers to continue growing.

Grabbling taters with a potato fork. *Tipper Pressley.*

To feast on new potatoes, gently scrape the thin skin. Don't try to remove it all—what remains will add a bit of delicious crunch or texture to the finished dish. Small potatoes don't need to be cut, but if your new potatoes are already rather large, cut into pieces about the size of a golf ball. Boil potatoes in salted water until they are barely fork tender. Do not overcook. Remove potatoes from water and allow to drain well. Heat butter or bacon grease in a cast-iron skillet on medium high. Once pan is hot, add new potatoes, turning during cooking so as to brown all sides. The browning process also works well by placing the pan in a hot oven.

TIP: New potatoes go especially well with soup beans, cornbread and kilt lettuce.

—Jim Casada

Creamed Peas and New Potatoes

Both peas and potatoes have long been favorites in mountain gardens, and for many generations, the latter—thanks to a combination of productivity (you can grow a lot of potatoes in a relatively small space) and keeping qualities—was a staple vegetable, perhaps second only to corn in overall dietary importance. Fortuitously, green peas and potatoes reach the edible stage about the same time in late spring, and combining them in a delicious dish was commonplace. In today's world, you can buy new potatoes at any time of the year, and frozen English peas make the other part of the classic combo something that can be enjoyed through all seasons.

The "creamed" can be a bit misleading, since no cream, just milk, is involved in the dish. Keep in mind that this is a foodstuff, unlike so many, which tends to be lacking in salt. That's because there's no salt, other than the small amount present in salted butter, found in the ingredients. You can just add salt and pepper to taste if the amount suggested leaves the vegetable mix tasting bland.

> *12 new potatoes, medium-sized*
> *1 cup fresh or frozen garden peas*
> *1 tablespoon salted butter*
> *2 tablespoons diced sweet onion*
> *1 tablespoon all-purpose flour*
> *1 cup whole milk*
> *1 teaspoon salt*
> *Ground black pepper*

Scrub potatoes with a vegetable brush to remove skin or else wash carefully and leave skin intact. Cut in half, unless some are quite small. Mixed sizes will be the case with those dug from the garden, while grocery store ones will have relative uniformity. Place in a saucepan in enough boiling water to cover and cook until barely tender (about 10 to 12 minutes—you can test with the point of a sharp knife), drain in a colander and set aside. Cook peas in another saucepan of boiling water (required time will be less, perhaps 5 minutes) and drain and set aside as well.

Melt butter in a large skillet and add onion in medium heat, cooking until translucent. At that point, add flour, stirring constantly with a whisk, and cook for a minute or so. Then slowly add milk, again stirring all the while, until everything is well combined. At this point, add peas, potatoes, salt and black pepper. Reduce heat to a slow simmer and allow to thicken until the sauce is slightly creamy. Adjust salt and pepper by taste testing, adding more if needed. Pour into a serving dish or bowl and enjoy. This makes a hearty main dish for an all-vegetable meal or a grand side dish with fried or roasted chicken.

—Jim Casada

"New" Potato Salad

There's something particularly appealing about the texture and taste of new potatoes. Here's an easy-peasy way to make a potato salad, liberally laced with boiled eggs, and it's fit for the pickiest of appetites.

3–6 boiled eggs, chopped
New potatoes, roughly 3 times the volume of eggs
½–1 cup sweet pickles, coarsely chopped (amount depends on how much you enjoy their taste)
Mustard and mayonnaise to taste (make sure you have enough to make the salad creamy)
1 teaspoon dried dill weed or 1 tablespoon fresh dill, finely chopped
Salt and pepper to taste
Paprika

Boil eggs and set aside when done. While they are boiling, cut potatoes into chunks and boil in a second pot until just tender. Drain and set aside. Peel and chop the eggs. Place eggs and potatoes in a large bowl, add the sweet pickles and then stir in mustard, mayonnaise, dill weed, salt and pepper. Sprinkle the finished potato salad with a really hefty dusting of paprika and place the bowl in the fridge to chill.

TIP: If you like raw onion, chop up a large Vidalia onion and add it to the bowl.

—Jim Casada

Asparagus Casserole

Much like the situation with rhubarb, asparagus is a perennial normally relegated to a location where it can be productive year after year with minimal care—occasional infusions of manure, weeding combined with mulching to allow it to grow without competition and due diligence to avoid disturbing the roots come plowing time. A properly maintained asparagus bed will remain productive for many years, and the tender shoots offer a springtime treat of sheer joy. Whether stewed with a bit of butter, steamed, grilled, coated in olive oil and prepared in the air fryers that have of late become all the rage or as the central ingredient in a casserole (the recipe offered here), asparagus is an upscale vegetable that does wonderfully well in high-country gardens.

30 spears of fresh asparagus (or one large can)
3 hard-boiled eggs, sliced
1 cup grated sharp cheddar cheese

White Sauce
2 tablespoons flour
2 tablespoons butter
¼ teaspoon salt
¼ teaspoon black pepper
1 ½ cups evaporated milk

Blend flour, butter, salt, black pepper and evaporated milk. Cook in a double boiler, stirring until thickened and smooth. Alternate layers of asparagus, eggs, cheese and sauce. Bake in a 350-degree oven for 20 minutes.

—Jim Casada

Kilt Lettuce
Each spring, I look forward to the first kilt lettuce of the season. Various names are used for the traditional Appalachian dish: killed lettuce, kill lettuce, wilted lettuce, lettuce and onions, killed salad or the word kilt used here.

Leaf lettuce
Green onions
Salt and pepper
Hot grease

Kilt lettuce should be served immediately after making. The dish uses fresh leaf lettuce from the garden or branch lettuce that grows wild along the creek. The way Granny taught me was to begin by picking and washing leaves of lettuce, making sure to dry off as much water as possible. Sometimes I wash mine early in the morning and leave it drying on a towel in the fridge.

Cut up several green onions, including tops, and mix with torn lettuce in a bowl, adding salt and pepper to taste. Pour hot bacon or streaked meat (salt pork) grease over the mixture. Be prepared for lots of hissing and popping when the grease hits the lettuce. Toss and serve quickly. It doesn't take much grease; a little goes a long way.

TIP: Kilt lettuce goes wonderfully with cornbread and soup beans.

—Tipper Pressley

Roasted Beets

Beets
Olive oil
Salt
Pepper

Peel and chop fresh beets. Toss with olive oil and turn out onto baking sheet. Season with salt and pepper to taste. Roast in 450-degree oven for 20 minutes or until tender.

TIP: For added sweetness, drizzle honey atop the beets before roasting.

—Tipper Pressley

Creamed Greens

Spinach or other greens
Olive oil or butter

Salt
Pepper
Nutmeg (optional)
Heavy cream

Cook spinach in oil or butter for a few minutes. Add additional butter or oil, salt, pepper and nutmeg to taste. Pour in heavy cream. The amount depends on the quantity of spinach you're working with, but it takes only a few tablespoons. Allow spinach to cook until it thickens slightly.

A skillet of creamed spinach.
Tipper Pressley.

TIP: Garlic or onions may also be added.

—Tipper Pressley

Chapter 11

THE BOUNTY OF SUMMER

When mountain gardens are laid by and the fruits of weeks of labor begin to cascade down in a glorious fashion formed by daily harvests, work transitions from the garden to canning, freezing or otherwise processing. It also means a veritable embarrassment of riches in terms of food choices. For both of us, this has traditionally been the time of year, more than any other, when vegetables reign supreme on the family table and when meals often are meatless or maybe just have some kind of meat gravy.

Zucchini Pie

2 teaspoons mustard (optional)
Unbaked pie shell
4 cups thinly sliced zucchini
1 cup chopped onion
¼ cup plus 1 tablespoon butter
2 teaspoons chopped parsley
½ teaspoon salt
¼ teaspoon garlic powder
½ teaspoon pepper

½ teaspoon basil
2 eggs
8 ounces shredded mozzarella cheese

Spread mustard on bottom of pie crust and set aside. Cook zucchini, onion and butter for 10 minutes until tender and beginning to become translucent. Stir in parsley, salt, garlic powder, pepper and basil. Combine eggs and cheese and add to zucchini mixture. Stir well and pour into prepared crust. Bake at 375 for 20 minutes or until lightly browned. Let stand 10 minutes before serving.

NOTE: While virtually all the recipes in this cookbook come from one of the authors or their families, this one is courtesy of Mary McLaren.

Fried Green Tomatoes

Cornmeal
Salt and pepper to taste
Egg
Milk
Cooking oil
Sliced green tomatoes

A batch of green tomatoes picked before first frost. *Tipper Pressley.*

Mix cornmeal, salt and pepper together in a shallow dish and set aside. Mix egg with milk in a second shallow dish. Heat oil to medium high. Drench tomato slices in liquid and then dredge in the cornmeal mix and fry in hot oil until golden brown on each side. Drain and serve immediately.

TIP: Be sure oil is piping hot before putting the tomato slices in it.

—Tipper Pressley

Squash and Onions

Squash
Onion
Butter or bacon grease
Salt and pepper to taste

Slice squash and onions in rounds. Melt butter or bacon grease in pan. Add squash and onions, seasoning with salt and pepper to taste. Cook until tender. A very quick and simple recipe that is served often in Appalachia.

—Tipper Pressley

Fried Corn

Fresh corn on the cob—at least one ear for each person
Bacon grease
Sugar to taste—it's really not necessary if using sweet corn
Water

Cut corn off cob and fry in bacon grease. Add a little water to pan to keep corn from sticking and, if desired, add sugar to taste. Cook corn while stirring for 10 minutes or until done.

NOTE: Corn plays a huge role in Appalachian foodways, and this recipe offers a quick variation to use when corn comes in each summer.

TIP: Butter may be used in place of bacon grease.

—Tipper Pressley

Roasted Okra

For folks who can never get past the "slimy" feel of stewed okra or those who want an alternative to the fried version of this dandy vegetable, roasting can be the way to go. Here's a delightfully different way to enjoy it.

2 tablespoons olive oil
2 tablespoons balsamic vinegar
2 pounds okra (the smaller the pods, the better; for larger ones,
cut into 1-inch lengths)
Salt to taste

Preheat oven to 425 degrees. Lightly grease a baking pan. Combine olive oil with balsamic vinegar in a large bowl. Add the okra to the bowl and toss until lightly coated. Arrange in a single layer on the baking pan. Roast, shaking or stirring every 5 minutes for 10 to 15 minutes or until the okra is nicely browned.

—Jim Casada

Eggplant Parmesan

1 (or more) nice-size eggplants
Kosher salt
1 egg
Whole wheat saltine crackers, crushed fine
Olive oil
Mozzarella cheese
Parmesan cheese
Marinara sauce

Slice eggplants into ⅛-inch-thick sections and sprinkle with kosher salt on both sides. Place slices atop paper towels and then cover with paper towels. Allow to sit for at least 15 minutes. This will remove bitterness, which can sometimes be a problem with eggplant. Pat dry.

Beat egg with a bit of water; dip each eggplant slice in the beaten egg and then coat with crushed crackers. Brown the slices in olive oil on medium heat (high heat will burn the cracker crumbs). Remove the slices from the pan and add homemade marinara sauce (see recipe in chapter 12). Place eggplant slices back in the pan and sprinkle tops liberally with mozzarella and Parmesan. Cover the pan and simmer until tender (about 15 minutes).

—Jim Casada

Veggie Sandwiches

Don't forget that you can make some mighty fine dinner (that's the meal eaten in the middle of the day in the world in which I live) fixin's by using fresh vegetables to make sandwiches. A tomato and lettuce sandwich suits me quite well, although I'll readily admit a couple or three slices of fried bacon added to the sandwich is the culinary lace on the bride's pajamas. Similarly, cucumbers and cream cheese, or cukes and mayo, can provide a tasty sandwich. Or try tomatoes with pimiento cheese, either as a sandwich or atop saltine crackers. I can go through this kind of food like a dose of salts (although that might not be the best comparison when one is talking of food).

—Jim Casada

Holy Green Beans

Productive, easy to grow, good for the soil, wonderfully tasty and delightfully diverse, beans in many forms figure in the Appalachian diet to a degree of prominence matched only by corn, potatoes and pork. Pole beans, half runners, cutshorts, bunch beans and other types of beans provide green beans for cooking in the traditional fashion along with other means of preparation, such as leather britches and pickled beans. Then there are butter beans, October beans, all sorts of dried (or "winter" beans) and more. They are easily stored, lend themselves to all sorts of recipes and have always been an Appalachian favorite.

Although Momma never used the term, after her death, the family frequently referred to a big pot of green beans as "holy green beans." In other words, they had had the hell cooked out of them. I think we got the humorous yet accurate description from a wonderful lady, Beulah Suddereth, who helped out with some with household chores as Mom's health began to decline and continued to do so for Dad after his mate of many decades was gone.

Whatever the origin of the terminology, in our household, there was none of this modern "tender-crisp, cooked with a touch of olive oil" nonsense when it came to green beans. You "looked" your beans (checked them for bugs or pieces of trash), strung and broke them and put the beans in a big pot with plenty of water. Two or three slices of streaked meat were then added and the pot set on a burner. Once the water was brought to a rolling boil, Momma would reduce the heat and the beans would simmer, all the while absorbing some of the streaked meat's salty goodness, for hours. She would check occasionally and add water when needed, but otherwise, it was just a matter of letting time and heat work their wonders. Incidentally, much the same approach was used for cooking various types of dried beans, crowder peas, cabbage, mustard or turnip greens, poke salad (the final go-round, after it had been cooked and drained twice) and the like.

—Jim Casada

Fried Okra

Preheat the oven to 350 degrees. Slice up as much okra as you'd like to serve and toss it in a mixture of cornmeal and flour (more cornmeal than flour) that has been salted and peppered well. Heat a cast-iron frying pan and add enough oil or bacon grease to cover the bottom. Once the pan is piping hot, throw in the okra and cook for about 3 minutes. Try your best to turn the okra over and cook for another 3 minutes. I never manage to turn every piece over—I just give it a good try with a spatula. Put the pan in the preheated oven

A plate of fried okra. *Tipper Pressley.*

and cook for about 10 minutes and you'll have a perfect pan of fried okra to eat. The time in the oven seems to remove some of the grease.

TIP: Tossing your okra in a plastic bag with the cornmeal and flour makes quick work of coating the pieces.

—Tipper Pressley

Fried Cabbage

Butter or bacon grease
Diced onions
Chopped cabbage

A fine head of cabbage ready to harvest. *Jim Casada.*

Heat butter or bacon grease in a cast-iron pan. Add onions and cook until tender and slightly browned. Add cabbage and stir well. Cover while cooking—but stir frequently to prevent cabbage from scorching or burning. Cooking time depends on how soft you prefer your cabbage. For cabbage that still has a little crunch, it takes about 5 minutes.

NOTE: Cabbage can be grown as a spring crop or a fall crop throughout much of southern Appalachia, and accordingly, this recipe is equally appropriate to the chapter on autumn's offerings.

—Tipper Pressley

Fried Squash

Yellow squash
1 egg
Milk
Salt
Pepper
Cornmeal
Olive or vegetable oil

The typical way to cook squash in Appalachia is to fry it. The actual procedure of frying varies from cook to cook. My mother slices squash in circles, tosses it in cornmeal seasoned with salt and pepper and fries it in vegetable oil. As the squash cooks, she stirs it, and it becomes sort of a fried squash scramble.

My preferred method is to cut squash lengthways for larger pieces. Dip squash pieces in a mixture of egg, milk, salt and pepper. Dredge squash in cornmeal and fry in olive oil or vegetable oil, turning each piece as it browns.

TIP: Squash cooks very quickly, so the pan must be watched closely.

—Tipper Pressley

Ground Cherry Salsa

Some Mexican restaurants feature salsa made with tomatillos (Moe's Southwest Grill offers it as a standard condiment or side). A first cousin to the tomatillo, the humble ground cherry, is often a volunteer in Appalachian gardens that returns year after year. Oddly enough, both are in the same family as deadly nightshade (so too, I believe, are tomatoes and eggplants). At any rate, for those who have ground cherries, turning them into something other than a casual snack when doing late summer and early fall garden work is both logical and easy. If the husk-covered globes have dropped from the plant, whether yellow (an indication they'll be slightly sweet) or not, they are ready for salsa.

Just remove the husks and mix them with your salsa ingredients of choice—tomatoes, onions, hot peppers and the like—and either run through a blender on a coarse setting or, to avoid quite as much mushiness, chop fine. Incidentally, an ulu is a great tool for this, and if you don't own one of these Inuit-type knives, I highly recommend acquiring one. Served with chips, plain bagels or even toast points, the salsa is scrumptious and oh-so-easy to make. Incidentally, mixed with some crowder peas or pinto beans, or maybe with some corn cut from the cob thrown in for good measure, it works perfectly well with cornbread salad (see chapter 1).

—Jim Casada

Squash Casserole

3 pounds yellow squash, sliced
5 tablespoons butter, divided
1 small onion, chopped
1 cup cheddar cheese
2 large eggs, lightly beaten
¼ cup mayonnaise
2 teaspoons sugar
1 teaspoon salt
20 round buttery crackers, crushed

Cook squash in boiling water until barely tender. Drain well. Melt 4 tablespoons butter in pan; add onion and cook until tender—about 5 minutes or so. Stir squash, cheese, eggs, mayonnaise, sugar and salt into onions. Spoon mixture into a greased 11" × 7" baking dish. Melt the rest of the butter and mix with crumbled crackers. Sprinkle on top of casserole. Bake at 350 degrees for 30 to 35 minutes or until done.

—Tipper Pressley

Chapter 12

THE MATCHLESS TOMATO

C orn may be the bastion of Appalachian foodstuffs, thanks to its incredible versatility, but tomatoes arguably come a close second when viewed from the perspective of just how welcome they are in the regional diet. They come in a variety of shapes, tastes and textures, not to mention almost infinite varieties. There are paste tomatoes and taste-laced tommytoes (the mountain name for miniature or cherry tomatoes); heirloom varieties and canning tomatoes; determinate or indeterminate growth patterns; and colors ranging from cream to almost black with pink, yellow and even striped versions figuring in the overall picture. They form

A basket of Lemon Boy tomatoes. *Jim Casada.*

the basis for countless dishes, from soups to stews and from Tex-Mex to Mediterranean cuisine; can make a simple sandwich a sampling of culinary heaven; lend themselves to canning, drying or freezing; can be eaten green as well as ripe; form a basic ingredient in various types of relish and pickles; and much, much more.

No mountain garden is complete without a row or two of stakes supporting tomatoes, and no cookbook on the region can overlook this favorite foodstuff. The recipes shared here are but a tiny sampling of ways in which tomatoes can be prepared and served. "Maters" are so much a part of Appalachian foodways that it is difficult to conceive of going more than a day or two without them figuring into the menu in one fashion or another.

Old-Time Tomato Sandwich

Including a recipe for a sandwich may seem an exercise in the obvious, but there are few things more satisfying than this one. A tomato sandwich made with a still-warm tomato fresh from the garden is a mighty fine thing. The first tomato sandwich of the summer is an annual cause for celebration in the mountains of Appalachia.

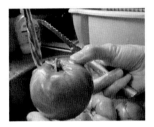

Canning tomatoes for the coming months. *Katie Pressley.*

Light bread
Mayonnaise
Salt
Pepper
Garden-fresh tomato slices

TIP: Variations on this most basic of homemade sandwiches are numerous—add bacon or bacon and lettuce, adorn with a slice of cheese, substitute a thin layer of pimiento cheese for mayonnaise and the like.

—Tipper Pressley

Granny's Tomato-Cucumber Salad

Tomato, diced
Onion, diced
Cucumber, diced
Salt and pepper to taste

Granny's tomato and cucumber salad. *Tipper Pressley.*

Toss all ingredients together in a bowl. Season with salt and pepper and chill for several hours before serving. All those great flavors of summer marry together into a sort of relish. Granny always said it made all the other food on the table taste better, and I agree with her. This simple salad adds brightness to a meal that might otherwise be bland.

TIP: A dash of apple cider vinegar gives this salad an additional kick.

—Tipper Pressley

Tomato Salsa

In the heat of summer, when tomatoes are abundant but thoughts of dealing with an oven or stove cause dismay, here's a grand way to use fresh tomatoes.

2 or 3 large tomatoes, diced
¼ cup finely chopped chives
½ cup pimento stuffed olives, chopped
1 garlic clove, minced
1 tablespoon red wine vinegar
3 tablespoons olive oil
Salt and pepper to taste

Combine the ingredients in a plastic or glass bowl, whisk gently and let stand in the refrigerator for 30 to 45 minutes.

TIP: Fresh mozzarella makes a nice addition to this salsa, and the pairing forms an ideal accompaniment to grilled burgers.

—Jim Casada

Grilled Tomatoes

Cut away the bottom end of your favorite tomato (to my way of thinking, you can't beat a Cherokee Purple), remove any core that is left and place top-side down on a barbecue grill or in the oven. Once the tomato starts to sizzle, sprinkle liberally with grated Parmesan cheese and continue cooking until the cheese melts and shows a bit of brown.

—Jim Casada

Homemade Marinara Sauce

90 small tomatoes or 60 medium tomatoes
2 tablespoons olive oil
3 medium onions
7 medium garlic cloves, minced
Large handful fresh oregano and basil (or 1 tablespoon each dried)
¼ cup sugar
2½ tablespoons kosher salt (or to taste)
Lots of fresh ground pepper (to taste)

Blanch and peel the tomatoes. Heat olive oil in a large saucepan. Add the onions and garlic and sauté until translucent. Add the remaining ingredients and bring the sauce to a boil. After it reaches a boil, reduce heat and simmer for about 2 hours or until nicely thickened. With a blender or immersion blender, blend the tomatoes on a low setting until smooth. Use at once or freeze for future meals.

Marinara sauce made with homegrown tomatoes may not look quite as red as store-bought versions, but it far outshines them when it comes to taste. It's a great way to use surplus tomatoes, and come cold weather, you'll relish spaghetti, chicken Parmesan, pizza, ziti or any of dozens of other dishes calling for marinara sauce. For that matter, a nice serving of pasta and marinara sauce makes mighty fine eating.

—Jim Casada

Tomato Dill Soup

1 stick butter
1½ large onions, pureed in a food processor
¼ cup minced fresh garlic
1½ teaspoons dried dill
¼ tablespoon kosher salt
⅛ tablespoon black pepper
9 cups (2 28-ounce cans plus 1 14½-ounce can) tomatoes (crushed or diced)
3 cups water
2 cups heavy cream (a pint of half-and-half with some whole milk added will also work)

Place butter, onions, garlic, dill, salt and black pepper in a large pot and cover. Sauté on low heat until onions are translucent. Add tomatoes and water. Simmer for 1 to 2 hours. Remove from heat and blend in cream.

—Jim Casada

Tomato Topper

2 tablespoons olive oil
2 teaspoons lemon juice
1 teaspoon dried basil
Salt and pepper to taste
4 fresh tomatoes, finely chopped
1 sweet onion, finely chopped

Mix olive oil, lemon juice, basil, salt and pepper with a wire whisk and pour atop diced tomatoes and onion. Toss and serve atop burgers, as a topping for toast points or as a side dish.

—Jim Casada

Tomato Pie

6 to 8 tomatoes
Salt
2 cups sharp cheddar (Cabot Seriously Sharp is a good choice)
¾ cup real mayonnaise
I small onion, sautéed in oil
Fresh basil
Pre-baked individual phyllo shells

Slice tomatoes fairly thin and lay them atop paper towels. Salt the tops and let sit 10 minutes before patting dry.

For the topping, shred cheddar, then mix with mayonnaise, adding salt and pepper to taste (remember that the tomatoes have been salted, and even though the patting will remove some of it, a salty tang will remain). In each phyllo shell, layer tomatoes, then onion and basil, then another tomato layer and spread topping to fill shell to the top. Bake at 375 degrees for 30 or so minutes or until done.

—Jim Casada

Chapter 13

ROOT CROPS

A couple of generations ago, an Appalachian garden without "taters," or a main meal without this amazingly versatile root crop, was almost unimaginable. This staple of the regional diet remains of critical importance. As one commenter on Tipper's blog put it, "As long as you have a tater, you have a banquet." Or in the words of Jim's Grandpa Joe, "Eat taters; they'll stick to a man's ribs." After all, most of those residing in the region had Scots-Irish roots, and a notable though often overlooked aspect of that background was heavy dietary reliance on root crops. The massive migration of Irish settlers as a result of the potato famine of the 1840s is well known, but the Great Famine did not have that marked an impact on the southern Appalachians. Most of those who settled the area, while often having roots in the British Isles, immigrated earlier.

Still, these hardy pioneers' utilization of Irish and sweet potatoes, along with other root crops such as turnips, onions and carrots, was extensive. Additionally, other root vegetables, including parsnips, leeks, beets, radishes, kohlrabi and Jerusalem artichokes, also entered the picture with some frequency. One of the great advantages of most root crops was that they kept well, and—with proper storage or, in some cases, just mounding or covering them where they grew—it was possible to have root crops available right through the winter. Strings of onions and bins filled with potatoes or turnips covered with straw were an integral part of the food picture on Appalachian homeplaces.

Gideon Laney and Rosie Duckworth with a mound of just-harvested potatoes. *Courtesy of Hunter Library, Western Carolina University.*

Cheese Potatoes

4 large potatoes sliced into fairly thin French fries
Salt and pepper to taste
1 small can (5 ounces) evaporated milk
1 cup shredded cheddar cheese
½ stick butter

Lay potatoes in the bottom of a baking pan; a 9" × 13" pan works well. Season to taste. Pour evaporated milk over potatoes; sprinkle with cheese. Cut butter into pieces and add to top of cheese. Bake uncovered at 400 for 25 to 30 minutes or until done.

TIP: Sprinkle parsley on before baking for a prettier presentation.

—Tipper Pressley

Soupy Potatoes

Potatoes
Water
Salt
Pepper
Butter

Soupy potatoes are a mainstay of the diet found in the Appalachian Mountains. Peel potatoes and quarter. Cover with water and add salt, pepper and butter to taste. Stew until desired tenderness is reached.

—Tipper Pressley

Candied Sweet Potatoes

4 pounds sweet potatoes (about 8 medium ones),
peeled and sliced into 1-inch-thick rounds
½ cup brown sugar, packed
4 tablespoons butter
¾ teaspoon salt
¼ teaspoon black pepper
Pinch nutmeg
¼ cup water

Place sweet potatoes and enough water to cover them in a saucepot; heat to boiling over high heat; reduce to low, cover and simmer for 5 minutes or until potatoes are barely fork tender. Drain; place potatoes in a 2-quart casserole. Heat brown sugar, butter, salt, pepper, nutmeg and water until butter melts—about 3 minutes—stirring often. Pour over sweet potatoes. Bake at 400 degrees uncovered for 40 minutes, stirring about halfway through. Potatoes should be tender and slightly browned.

Candied sweet potatoes ready to serve. *Tipper Pressley.*

—Tipper Pressley

Fried Onions

Onions are well loved in Appalachia. From seasoning other dishes to being cooked up in a medicinal fashion, they are used in many ways. One of the simplest approaches to preparing onions is to slice them and fry them in butter or bacon grease until they are tender and brown around the edges. Slow and long cooking is the trick to getting wonderful, deep color and flavor. Fried onions can be eaten as a side dish; used as a topping for hamburgers, hot dogs or other meats; or even served with scrambled eggs. They are often fried together with sliced potatoes.

—Tipper Pressley

Baked Onions with Cheese

5 to 8 onions, sliced thin
Salt and pepper to taste
3 tablespoons butter
3 tablespoons water
Shredded cheese

Add sliced onions to a greased baking dish. Season with salt and pepper. Dot with butter. Sprinkle with water. Cover dish and bake at 400 degrees for about 30 to 40 minutes or until the onions are tender. During final 10 minutes of cooking, top with shredded cheese and remove cover.

—Tipper Pressley

Stewed Turnips

Turnips are often grown in the gardens of Appalachia. An easy, quick way to use them is offered in this recipe.

Turnips
Water
Salt
Pepper
Butter

A batch of freshly pulled turnips.
Tipper Pressley.

Quarter turnips, cover with water and add salt, pepper and butter to taste. Stew until your desired tenderness is reached.

TIP: If the turnips are woody or tough on the outside, they will need to be peeled prior to cooking.

—Tipper Pressley

Mustard Greens and Turnips

1 peck greens
2 or 3 turnips
2 slices streaked meat
Salt and pepper to taste

Wash a big bait of greens fresh from the garden, being sure to give them multiple rinses to remove all dirt and grit. If they are overly large, it is best to remove the stems. Chop up two or three turnips in small pieces

Harvesting a mess of mustard greens.
Tipper Pressley.

(diced is best). Place greens and turnips in a large pot with plenty of water. Throw in a couple of slices of streaked meat and bring to a boil. Reduce to a simmer and allow to cook until greens and turnips are done. Add salt and pepper to taste. Serve piping hot.

A picking of greens. *Tipper Pressley*

Be sure to save the cooking liquid (often called pot likker, although strictly speaking, pot likker is a cabbage-based dish). It makes for mighty fine eating when you dip a chunk of cornbread in it or, as Grandpa Joe used to do, pour it in a bowl and crumble cornbread over the rich, vitamin-filled juice. Turnip greens can also be cooked this way, but my personal preference is for mustard. Collards are the green of choice here in South Carolina where I now live, but you can have my part of them.

—Jim Casada

Roasted Potatoes

Roasting potatoes offers a different way of serving this Appalachian staple, and they go well with about any meal as a hearty side dish.

1 large or 2 small potatoes per person
Vegetable oil
Salt and pepper

Carefully scrub the potatoes; leave the skin on. Slice in rounds about ¼ inch thick. Coat lightly with vegetable oil and place on a cookie sheet. Sprinkle with salt and pepper and place in a 375-degree oven. Cook for 10 minutes or so and check to see if the sides of the slices touching the cookie sheet are brown. If so, use a spatula or tongs to turn; otherwise, cook a bit longer. Continue cooking until slices are nicely browned and slightly crisp on both sides and mealy in the middle. Serve piping hot.

NOTE: Leftovers can be saved and reheated in a frying pan for a side dish with breakfast.

—Jim Casada

Potato Soup

Throughout much of Appalachia, the standard remedy when someone has the mollygrubs (feels poorly) is not chicken soup but potato soup. Rich and savory, it's easily prepared and a welcome dish—if you're sick or not—especially in cold weather.

Peeled potatoes (figure 1 or 2 per person)
1 large sweet onion
½ stick butter
1 cup chicken broth or stock
2 cups whole milk
Salt and pepper to taste
Fresh chives, bacon bits or grated cheddar cheese (optional)

Cut potatoes into ¼-inch slices and boil until they break apart readily. Meanwhile, as potatoes are cooking, slice onion and sauté in a pan with half of the butter until translucent. Drain most of the water from the potatoes, then add broth, onion, milk, remaining butter and seasonings to a large pot. Stir while reheating. Serve piping hot. Serves 4 to 6.

TIPS:
1. If desired, you can gussy up the soup by sprinkling with fresh chives, crumbling bacon bits atop individual servings or garnishing with grated cheddar cheese. Leftovers reheat well.
2. For a really rich soup, use half-and-half instead of milk.

—Jim Casada

Simple Baked Potatoes

When it comes to satisfying food simplicity, a properly baked potato is mighty hard to beat. But not all baked potatoes are equal. Microwaving gives you edibles in a hurry, but the skin won't have the crusty crunch that is so satisfying. Much the same holds true if you use aluminum wrap and bake your tubers in the oven. Yet a couple of simple tricks of the tater trade can make a world of difference. Here's the traditional route to success.

Left: Newly dug potatoes waiting on the ground. *Jim Casada.*

Below: A bountiful handful of spring radishes. *Katie Pressley.*

Left: Cornmeal-coated squash fried to a golden brown. *Tipper Pressley.*

Below: A handful of ripe, husked ground cherries. *Jim Casada.*

Right: Red okra tastes the same as green, but its striking color adds visual appeal on the stalk or before cooking.
Tipper Pressley.

Below: A hefty harvest of morel mushrooms.
Jim Casada.

A sprawling patch of ramps promises a springtime feast. *Don Casada.*

Red Delicious apples ready for picking. *Jim Casada.*

Right: A simple, one-man cider press squeezes out a run of apple cider. *Jim Casada.*

Below: A batch of newly gathered apples spread out on a mountain porch prior to being worked up. *Tipper Pressley.*

A cluster of pawpaws at harvesttime. *Jim Casada.*

Vines laden with blackberries just beginning to ripen. *Jim Casada.*

Mulberry juice. *Tipper Pressley.*

Biscuits, butter and jelly—an enduring Appalachian treat. *Tipper Pressley.*

Left: Canning bread-
and-butter pickles.
Corie Graddick.

Below: Shelves
laden with colorful
canning jars
holding summer's
rich bounty.
Tipper Pressley.

Freshly gathered pears waiting to be worked up. *Tipper Pressley.*

Punch bowl cake. *Tipper Pressley.*

Open-faced blackberry pie. *Tipper Pressley.*

A maypop (or passionflower) bloom. *Tipper Pressley.*

Left: A loaf of pecan-studded zucchini bread. *Tipper Pressley.*

Below: A traditional southern Appalachia breakfast— country ham, redeye gravy, biscuits, eggs and grits. *Tipper Pressley.*

Summer's rich bounty for supper. *Tipper Pressley.*

Robert Scoville frying trout streamside in Pisgah National Forest. *Jim Casada.*

Making a pan of sausage gravy. *Tipper Pressley.*

A native persimmon tree laden with fruit in early autumn. *Jim Casada.*

Left: A fine field of corn with mountains in the background. *Tipper Pressley.*

Below: A Buchanan family picnic. *Courtesy Hunter Library, Western Carolina University.*

Above: Honeybees busy on corn tassels. *Don Casada.*

Right: A near-ripe apple hangs from a tree in late summer. *Tipper Pressley.*

An Appalachian homestead and its adjacent garden. *Don Casada.*

Susan Casada in her family's garden. *Don Casada.*

1 baking potato per person
Vegetable oil
Butter
Coarse sea salt

Thoroughly wash and scrub the potatoes—high-starch ones, such as the old Appalachian favorite, Kennebec, or store-bought Russets, are best. Dry the potatoes and coat thoroughly with vegetable oil. Place potatoes on a baking sheet and sprinkle liberally with coarse sea salt, turning so all sides are well salted. Bake at 400 degrees for about an hour—time will depend on the size of the potatoes—until fully done. You can check by holding one in an oven mitt and squeezing it gently. If it yields, the potato is ready to eat. The end result of baking potatoes in this fashion will be a crisp skin enclosing inner goodness just begging to be popped open and loaded with real butter.

TIP: Through the addition of ingredients such as sour cream, shredded cheese, chopped green onions, chives, bits of dried cayenne pepper, bacon crumbles, fried streaked meat morsels or other goodies, a large baked potato can become a meal. This is especially true with a salad as a side dish.

—Jim Casada

Roasted Carrots

Carrots
Oil (olive oil works particularly well)
Salt and pepper to taste

Scrub or peel carrots and chop to desired size. Toss with oil and season with salt and pepper. Lay carrots out in a single layer on a baking sheet. Roast at 400 degrees for 20 minutes.

TIP: Baby carrots can be left whole.

—Tipper Pressley

Carrot Salad

1 cup carrots, grated
1 large apple, diced
1 cup celery, chopped
1 green or red pepper, chopped
Mayonnaise
Salt and pepper to taste

A raw carrot salad. *Tipper Pressley.*

Toss the first four ingredients together. Add mayonnaise to taste. Season with salt and pepper to taste.

TIP: This salad may be altered by increasing or decreasing ingredients according to individual preference.

—Tipper Pressley

Carrot, Raisin and Pineapple Salad

1 cup grated carrots, chopped with an ulu or knife
½ cup raisins
½ cup canned pineapple slices or chunks, drained and cut into small pieces
Mayonnaise

Stir the carrots, raisins and pineapple together and then mix in mayonnaise to taste (do not use too much). A pinch of sugar can be added if desired, and for extra crunch and a taste difference, the same is true of chopped pecans.

TIP: For a color-consistent salad, use golden raisins.

—Jim Casada

Pecan Crunch Sweet Potatoes

1 stick butter
2 eggs
2 teaspoons vanilla
1 cup sugar
3 cups sweet potatoes, cooked and mashed

Combine butter, eggs, vanilla and sugar. Add to mashed sweet potatoes and spread mixture in a baking dish.

Topping
⅓ stick butter, melted
1 cup brown sugar
2 tablespoons flour
1 cup finely chopped pecans

Mix topping ingredients and crumble over potatoes.

Bake at 350 degrees for 25 to 30 minutes or until bubbly and golden brown. This has long been a traditional dish at Casada family gatherings.

—Jim Casada

Chapter 14
FALL AND WINTER VEGETABLES

W hile there is quite an array of vegetables associated with cool or cold weather in the southern Appalachians, squash hold pride of place. When one thinks of squash, they basically fall into two categories—summer squash and winter squash. Both have long been important in the Appalachian diet. Native Americans introduced many members of the squash family to early settlers, and that was especially true of long-keeping winter squash such as pumpkins. As part of the traditional "three sisters" pattern of agriculture, pumpkins, cushaws, candy roasters and other "keeping" squash could, once established with a good start, pretty well look after themselves as they sprawled across a corn patch and used their large leaves and wide-ranging vines to hold most competing vegetation at bay. Winter squash furnished pies and breads as well as being eaten on their own. Summer squash (which have already been covered earlier) such as yellow crooknecks, zucchini and pattypans could be fried, stewed, used in soup mixes, served as a key ingredient in succotash and savored in other ways. For their part, winter squash enjoyed the distinct advantage of keeping well. When stored in a dark, cool root cellar or amid a bed of straw beneath a protective corn shock, they lasted well into winter or even into spring.

Squash formed frequent table fare for most Appalachian folks and were, along with "keeper" root crops, particularly important during the period from autumn's first killing frost until the earliest greens became available the

A plow horse and a trio of women plant a field in potatoes. *Courtesy of Hunter Library, Western Carolina University.*

following spring. There were, however, a few other cold-hardy vegetables to be enjoyed for much of the fall—if, indeed, not on into winter. The recipes that follow offer a glimpse into this wide-reaching culinary tableau, and keep in mind that there are recipes for dessert or sweet preparations for many of the fall/winter foodstuffs in other chapters.

Cushaw Soup

1 ½ cups water
1 ½ cups chicken stock
5 cups cushaw or other winter squash, peeled and cubed
1 medium potato, peeled and cubed
1 teaspoon salt
⅓ cup heavy cream

Combine water and chicken stock in a saucepot and add squash, potato and salt. Cook for about 45 minutes at a simmer until vegetables are soft. Mash vegetables with potato masher or spoon to desired consistency. Add cream and cook for 3 minutes. Goes wonderfully well with a cake of cornbread.

NOTE: This soup keeps very well in the refrigerator and is as good warmed up as when it was first made.

TIP: Cooked soup can also be blended for a smoother consistency.

—Tipper Pressley

Coleslaw

Cabbage is one of the relatively rare three-season vegetables (which can be grown or survive in the garden in every season except winter) in the Appalachians. From when it first becomes available in the spring onward, it looms large in regional diet. Cabbage heads keep well when harvested and last into summer if simply left in the garden, and second plantings for fall are possible throughout most of the region. Indeed, in the North Carolina mountains that are our homeland, cabbage has long been a traditional fall crop widely grown for market. When it comes to making coleslaw, one of the most common uses for cabbage, there are as many variations to the dish as there are stars in the sky. Here's my simple version, one our family greatly enjoys.

Cabbage
Salt and pepper to taste
Sour cream
Mayonnaise
Splash of milk
Dash of sugar

Shred cabbage and place in a large bowl. Season with salt and pepper. Mix desired amounts of sour cream and mayonnaise along with milk and sugar in a small bowl. I aim for twice as much mayonnaise as sour cream. Pour mixture over cabbage and toss well. Allowing the coleslaw to marry in the fridge for several hours improves the flavor.

TIP: Shredded carrots and finely minced onion can be added to this simple coleslaw recipe for additional flavor and color.

—Tipper Pressley

Butternut Squash Soufflé

3 cups butternut squash, cooked and pureed (pumpkin and cushaw work equally well)
I cup sugar
3 eggs, beaten
½ cup milk
¼ cup butter
I tablespoon vanilla
I cup brown sugar
I cup chopped nuts
½ cup self-rising flour
¼ cup butter

Combine the first six ingredients and mix well. Pour into a buttered baking dish. Combine the rest of the ingredients, incorporating butter until you reach a coarse-crumb consistency. Sprinkle mixture on squash puree and bake at 350 degrees until top is brown (about 25 to 30 minutes).

NOTE: This recipe can be used as a sweet side dish, much like a sweet potato casserole, or as a dessert.

—Tipper Pressley

Winter Squash and Kale

This is a dandy recipe combining two winter vegetable stalwarts, squash and kale. Any type of winter squash can be used, but butternut squash works especially well. Amounts can vary depending on how many people you plan to serve.

135

Tipper Pressley with an armload of winter squash. *Corie Graddick.*

2 cups diced winter squash
1 to 2 tablespoons butter or vegetable oil
Salt and pepper to taste
2 handfuls chopped kale

Dice winter squash and sauté until tender in a mixture of butter and olive oil. Season to taste with salt, pepper and whatever other appropriate seasonings you enjoy. Once squash is tender—but not falling apart—remove from pan. Add a couple handfuls of chopped kale and cook for a few minutes. Additional butter or oil may be added before cooking kale if pan is quite dry. Once the greens are wilted, add the squash back to the pan and toss gently to combine the two.

TIP: This recipe makes a wonderful side dish to accompany most any meat or fish.

—Tipper Pressley

Savory Roasted Cushaw

5 or 6 cups cubed cushaw
4 tablespoons olive oil
Salt to taste
Pepper to taste
2 teaspoons dried rosemary (or use fresh, if you have it)
2 cloves minced garlic
2 tablespoons Parmesan cheese, grated

Heat oven to 400 degrees. Place cushaw on a large baking pan in one layer. Drizzle olive oil over cushaw and stir to coat. Sprinkle with salt and bake for 20 minutes. Take cushaw from oven and stir. Sprinkle cushaw with pepper, rosemary, garlic and Parmesan cheese. Put pan back in oven and bake until done, about 10 minutes longer.

—Tipper Pressley

Roasted Pumpkin Seeds

Having been raised by parents who reached early adulthood in the depths of the Depression and for whom frugality was a byword, I've always been a staunch adherent to the "waste not, want not" school of thinking. That certainly applies to drying and saving seeds rather than buying them and to utilizing the garden's bounty to its fullest.

A batch of pumpkin seeds.
Tipper Pressley.

Other recipes in this collection deal with pumpkin flesh, but it's a mistake to overlook the savory seeds inside this member of the winter squash family. The seeds are tasty and nutritious, and they make a fine snack.

To prepare pumpkin seeds, put them aside when you work up the pumpkin, and while it is roasting in the oven, separate the seeds from the stringy fiber to which they are attached. Save plenty for pumpkin planting in the next garden cycle (putting them in a small bag and storing them in the freezer assures viability) and then toast the rest.

To toast, lightly coat the cleaned seeds in cooking oil, spread them out atop a cookie sheet, sprinkle with salt and place in a 375-degree oven. Toast until they begin to show a hint of brown and then remove. The seeds can be eaten whole or, if you have the patience, cracked and the kernel removed. I eat them whole and figure that along with the fine taste, I'm getting some fiber.

—Jim Casada

Brown Sugar–Baked Acorn Squash

Easily grown in the home garden and readily available at the grocery store, acorn squash are much smaller than most types of winter squash (a single one is just right for two ample servings). This recipe is simple and requires little prep time.

1 acorn squash per two diners
¼ cup brown sugar per squash
Large pat of butter for each squash half

With a sturdy butcher knife, cut each squash in half lengthwise and use a spoon to scrape out the seeds and pulp. Lightly score the flesh, being sure you don't cut all the way through. Place the squash halves on a cookie sheet or in a baking dish. Place a pat of butter in each cavity and then pour the brown sugar over it. Bake at 400 degrees for 1 hour to 1 hour and 15 minutes or until squash is tender. Serve hot as either a sweet vegetable dish or dessert.

TIP: Molasses, cane syrup, maple syrup or honey can be substituted for brown sugar.

—Jim Casada

Chapter 15

VEGETABLES AND OTHER FOODS
FROM THE WILD

Historically, folks in Appalachia have made considerable use of wild vegetables. That was particularly true in early spring, when months of a diet sorely lacking in the nutritional needs fulfilled by vegetables led them to the fields and forest. Delicacies such as sochan, creasy greens, watercress, poke, ramps, branch lettuce, dandelions, chickweed, nettles and fiddlehead ferns were not only welcome, but they also served significant needs by providing certain vitamins as well as bringing dietary variety and being available for the gathering. Add mushrooms (especially morels), and you had a veritable panoply of goodness from the wilds.

Sautéed Chanterelles

Fresh chanterelle mushrooms, chopped roughly
Butter
Garlic
Salt
Pepper

Look chanterelles to make sure no bugs are hiding among the gills. Melt butter and add garlic to pan. Cook for 1 minute. Add mushrooms and season to taste with salt and pepper. Cook lightly until moisture from mushrooms has mostly evaporated and then serve.

—Tipper Pressley

Gathering chanterelle mushrooms. *Tipper Pressley.*

Sautéed Purslane

Purslane is a readily available weed in most areas. The easiest way to utilize this free, nutritious vegetable—which is considered a superfood—is to toss the tender, succulent leaves with other greens for a fresh salad. My favorite way to cook it is also simple and easy.

1 onion, diced
1 clove garlic, minced
1 medium tomato, diced
1 or 2 handfuls purslane, chopped

Dice up onion and cook in your favorite oil in a frying pan until it's just beginning to brown around the edges. Throw in garlic and let cook for another minute. Next, add tomato and purslane. Cook for 8 to 10 minutes and serve as a side dish.

Other vegetables can be added depending on what you have available or your personal preferences. I love to eat mine with cornbread, and it's especially good over rice.

A serving of sautéed purslane. *Corie Graddick.*

TIP: If you pick wild purslane away from home (it readily grows in home gardens), be sure it is not in an area that has been sprayed.

NOTE: The stems and flowers, as well as the leaves, are edible.

—Tipper Pressley

Dandelion Jelly

*1 quart dandelion flowers from an area that has
not been sprayed with chemicals
1 quart water
1 box powdered fruit pectin
4½ cups sugar
Sterilized jars, lids and rings*

A cluster of just-picked dandelion
blooms. *Tipper Pressley.*

Rinse flowers and add to quart of water.
Bring to a boil and boil for 3 minutes.
Drain liquid from flowers. Using a piece of
cheesecloth works well to get the tiny pieces out. Put strained liquid
in large pot. I typically end up with 4 cups of liquid after boiling and
straining the dandelions. Stir in pectin and let mixture come to a full
rolling boil. Once mixture boils, add sugar and stir well. Cook mixture
until it comes to another full boil. Boil for 1 minute. Quickly ladle hot
liquid into sterilized jars and seal.

TIP: If you don't have quite 4 cups of liquid, water or fruit juice may be
added to make up the difference.

—Tipper Pressley

Dandelion Greens

*½ gallon loose dandelion leaves per large serving (chop off the bottom portion
of tough or woody stems)
¼ onion, diced, per serving
3 or 4 tablespoons hot bacon grease*

Gather young dandelion leaves in early spring, making sure you know
they have not been sprayed. Wash leaves well and pat dry with a clean
towel or paper towels. Sauté diced onion in bacon grease until tender.
Add dandelion greens and cook until wilted—about 4 to 5 minutes.

TIP: Like other greens, cooked dandelion leaves wilt down to take up significantly less space than fresh ones, so remember that when judging the amount needed for a meal.

—Tipper Pressley

Violet Jelly

2 cups violet blooms from an area that has not been sprayed with chemicals
2 cups boiling water
1 box powdered fruit pectin
Juice of one lemon
4 cups sugar
Sterilized jars, lids and rings

Rinse blooms. Place in a glass bowl and pour 2 cups of boiling water over them. Cover bowl with plate and allow to sit on counter overnight. Drain liquid from violet blooms. Place violet juice, pectin and lemon juice in a large saucepot. Bring mixture to a boil. Once mixture boils, add sugar and stir well. Cook until it comes to another full boil. Boil for 1 minute. Quickly ladle hot liquid into sterilized jars and seal.

TIP: If you don't have quite 4 cups of liquid, water or fruit juice may be added to make up the difference.

—Tipper Pressley

Fried Ramps with Potatoes

Potatoes, diced
Ramps, chopped
Oil (vegetable oil, lard, olive oil or bacon grease)

Fry potatoes in your choice of oil. Once potatoes are nearly done, add chopped ramps and finish cooking.

Freshly harvested and cleaned ramps ready to cook. *Jim Casada.*

—Tipper Pressley

Ramps with Eggs

Butter or bacon grease
Ramps, chopped
Eggs

Add bacon grease to frying pan and heat to medium high. Cook ramps for a few minutes until tender. Add eggs and scramble. Serve with biscuits or toast.

—Tipper Pressley

Poke Sallet

1 gallon poke sprouts
2 or 3 pats melted butter or 3 tablespoons bacon grease
Salt and black pepper to taste
2 eggs (optional)

Gather a mess of tender poke sprouts (they are best when 3 to 5 inches high) and rinse thoroughly to remove any dirt. Place in a pot and bring the water to a rolling boil, then cool to a simmer before pouring the poke sallet and water into a colander to drain. Repeat the process at least once, preferably twice. The reason for doing this is that pokeweed is exceptionally rich in Vitamin A, so much so that it can be toxic unless you use this cook-and-drain process to remove some of the vitamin.

Next, place the drained poke in a skillet with a bit of melted butter or bacon grease. Heat until piping hot, add salt and black pepper to taste and serve immediately. Some folks like to garnish poke with chopped boiled eggs or break a couple of eggs into the greens when they are added to the skillet and stir until the eggs have cooked.

NOTE: A pone of cornbread or cathead biscuits goes mighty fine with poke sallet.

—Jim Casada

Sautéed Morels

Morel mushrooms are a great delicacy, and when sautéed, they retain all their delicate flavor. I have three favorite ways of preparing them in this manner. In each case, soak the mushrooms in cold water for 15 to 30 minutes and then look and clean them thoroughly. Inspect carefully, because critters like to crawl up inside the hollow mushrooms. There's almost always a bit of dirt to be dealt with as well. Dab dry with a towel or paper towels and slice each mushroom in half.

It is hard to beat introducing the mushroom pieces to simmering butter in a pan, sautéing until they begin to brown and eating them right from the pan. Put a few pats of butter (the real McCoy) in a large frying pan and melt it before adding the sliced morels. Simmer until the morels are cooked. They will shrink quite a bit and, thanks to the fact that they hold considerable moisture, you'll have lots of a juice/butter combination in the pan. You might want to save this flavorful broth to use in a morel soup or chowder (see below); I like to dip toast points in it.

Another approach is to beat up a couple of eggs and dip each mushroom piece in the resulting batter before putting them in hot butter to cook.

A third option is to crumble up saltine crackers, then use the same egg dip and follow with a coating of crushed saltines before putting the morels in the frying pan. Whatever your choice, it's food for the gods.

Eat the morels piping hot as an appetizer or as a side dish to scrambled eggs.

—Jim Casada

Morel Chowder

2 cups morels, cleaned and sliced
¼ cup chopped onion
1 cup peeled and diced potatoes
½ cup finely chopped celery

½ cup finely chopped carrots
4 tablespoons butter
2 tablespoons olive oil
I tablespoon flour
2 tablespoons cold water
2 cups chicken broth (or use the broth left from sautéed morels in combination
with chicken broth)
½ teaspoon salt
½ teaspoon black pepper
I cup whole milk
¼ cup freshly grated Parmesan cheese
Paprika

A bowl of morel chowder.
Jim Casada.

Clean and slice mushrooms; chop vegetables. Melt butter and add olive oil. Add onions and sauté until tender. Add mushrooms, potatoes, celery and carrots; cover and cook on medium heat for 15 to 20 minutes or until vegetables are tender. In a small bowl, thoroughly combine flour with cold water and slowly stir into vegetables. Add broth, salt and pepper until heated through. Add milk and Parmesan cheese and heat; do not boil. Serve immediately, topped with additional Parmesan cheese and paprika.

—Jim Casada

Morel Soup

I pound fresh morels, cleaned and sliced
I–2 tablespoons lemon juice
I large sweet onion, chopped
3 tablespoons butter (do not substitute margarine)
2 tablespoons all-purpose flour
4 cups whole milk
3 teaspoons chicken bouillon granules

½ teaspoon salt
⅛ teaspoon black pepper

Clean morels and sprinkle with lemon juice. Sauté in a saucepan with onion and butter until translucent and tender. Sprinkle with flour and stir thoroughly. Gradually add milk, bouillon, salt and pepper. Bring to a rolling boil, stirring vigorously as you do so, and continue stirring for 2 minutes. Reduce heat and simmer 10 to 15 minutes. If you like the taste of thyme, add ½ teaspoon to the recipe, but keep in mind that morels have a delicate flavor.

—Jim Casada

Chapter 16

DOMESTIC FRUITS

Widely cultivated as a cash crop, especially in higher elevations over much of Appalachia, apples have multiple virtues and hold pride of place among the fruits cultivated regionally. They keep well, come in many varieties, can be used in desserts as well as served as a side dish for the main part of a meal, lend themselves to preservation through both canning and drying and are healthy and delicious. Small family apple orchards were once commonplace (Jim's family had one, even though they lived on the outskirts of town), and fruit figured prominently in regional diet.

Clarence Shore's old-time fruit stand. *Courtesy of Hunter Library, Western Carolina University.*

While apples ruled as undisputed king among domestic fruits in the Appalachian South, others certainly have always enjoyed a significant place. Most self-sustaining farms or homesteads had not only apple trees but also peaches, one or two cherry trees (possibly both sweet and sour varieties), plums and both soft (eating) and hard (cooking) pears. The recipes that follow in this chapter are only part of the fruit picture, because many of the desserts and other sweets covered in subsequent chapters feature them as well.

Stewed Peaches

A bowl of blushing peaches.
Tipper Pressley.

3 cups sliced fresh peaches or 1 (16-ounce) bag frozen peaches
½ cup sugar
¼ cup water

Add all ingredients to saucepot and simmer for 10 minutes. Serve sliced cocoa bread with the peaches.

—Jim Casada

Spiced Pears

¼ cup water
⅓ cup brown sugar
¾ teaspoon cinnamon
¾ teaspoon nutmeg
2 cups soft (eating) pears, slices or halves

A sink full of pears ready to be worked up. *Tipper Pressley.*

Combine water, sugar and spices in a saucepot. Bring to a boil. Reduce heat and simmer for 5 minutes. Add pears to the pot and cook, stirring frequently, for another 5 minutes.

TIP: Spiced pears are wonderful with a slice of pound cake or as a side dish.

—Tipper Pressley

Fresh Pear Bread

3 cups all-purpose flour
1 teaspoon salt
1 teaspoon baking soda
2 teaspoons baking powder
2 teaspoons cinnamon
¾ cup vegetable oil
1½ cups sugar
3 eggs
1 teaspoon vanilla
4 cups finely chopped soft (eating) pears
1 cup chopped nuts (optional)

Stir together flour, salt, baking soda, baking powder and cinnamon. Set aside. Mix oil and sugar. Add eggs one at a time, beating well after each. Mix in vanilla. Gradually add the dry ingredients until just incorporated. Batter will be dry until pears are added. Add pears and nuts; stir to combine. Spoon into two greased or parchment-paper-lined loaf pans. Batter will be thick. Bake at 350 degrees for 1 hour or until done. If using greased pans, cool for 10 minutes for easier bread removal.

TIP: Drained canned pears may be substituted for fresh ones.

—Tipper Pressley

Applesauce Pancakes

There are endless ways to gussy up pancakes, but most involve dropping some type of fruit, berry, chocolate or the like onto the top of a pancake already on the griddle. This approach is a notable exception inasmuch as the fruit goes into the batter as it is being prepared.

1 cup your favorite store-bought pancake mix
2 eggs
1 tablespoon cooking oil

¼ stick butter, melted
2 cups applesauce
½ cup buttermilk or enough to make a
smooth batter

Blend all ingredients together by beating briskly with a whisk. If the batter is too stiff, add a bit more buttermilk; if it's too watery, add a bit more pancake mix. Pour pancakes atop a well-greased griddle. Turn only once.

Working up a batch of apples.
Tipper Pressley.

TIP: For a crunchy, nutty taste, add ½ cup chopped pecans.

—Jim Casada

Waldorf Salad

One of the most widely used ways of enjoying apples is in a Waldorf Salad. While the name might suggest it originated in the New York establishment of that name, such is unlikely to be the case. Never mind geographical origins; certainly, it is a fine way to enjoy fresh apples. In yesteryear, one of the standard ingredients, celery, wasn't readily available in rural Appalachia, but this is no longer the case.

½ cup or a bit less mayonnaise
Splash lemon juice
2 cups unpeeled sweet apples, cored and chopped into small pieces
¾ cup chopped celery
½ cup chopped black walnuts
½ cup raisins

Mix mayonnaise with lemon juice, and once they are suitably blended, add the rest of the ingredients and toss just enough to coat everything with the mayonnaise/lemon juice mixture.

TIP: Chopped pecans can be substituted for black walnuts, but they don't have the same bold and distinctive taste.

—Jim Casada

Canned Sweet Apples

For this recipe, sweet varieties such as Golden or Red Delicious, often styled "eating" apples, are ideal. More tart, "keeper" apples such as Staymans or Winesaps are also fine, but they will require more sugar.

½ bushel apples, peeled and sliced
10 cups sugar
2 or 3 tablespoons ascorbic acid color keeper or lemon juice, to avoid browning

After peeling and slicing apples and then treating with color keeper, cover with 10 cups of sugar and allow to sit overnight in the refrigerator.

After sitting overnight, cook apples in a large pot until tender. Between the sugar and the juice released from the apples, you probably won't need to add any water. Pack in hot jars and seal. Process for 15 minutes in a boiling water canner.

In both our homes, canned apples have long been a central and cherished dietary item. Served as a side dish, they were called sauce or sometimes just fruit. They aren't a true sauce, at least consistency-wise, but rather chunks of cooked apples.

Jars of newly canned apples.
Tipper Pressley.

TIP: A bowl of fruit from a jar, warmed and topped with a pat of butter and then adorned with a couple of crumbled sugar cookies, makes a dandy dessert.

—Jim Casada

Fried Apples

6 to 8 eating apples such as Red Delicious, Fuji, Golden Delicious or Gala varieties
¾ cup sugar
Generous pinch cinnamon (or a heaping teaspoon of tiny red heart cinnamon candy)
¼ stick butter

Core each apple and cut into eighths, leaving the skin intact. Place in a large stewpot and add sugar, cinnamon and butter. Heat until bubbling, stirring steadily with a wooden spoon, and then cut back to a simmer while continuing to stir. Cook until apples are completely soft. Depending on the variety, slices will remain intact or soften to the point of falling apart.

In truth, this process is one of stewing apples, but invariably they are described as fried. Smaller batches can actually be prepared in a frying pan. If the consistency of the peel bothers you, remove it before beginning to cook, but by doing so, you discard both taste and fiber.

—Jim Casada

Stewed Sour Cherries

John Walker with a batch of just-picked cherries. *Courtesy of the National Park Service.*

When I was a boy, we had a mammoth Montmorency cherry in the backyard that bore limb-bending quantities of fruit, predictably and prolifically, year after year. With the aid of a whole bunch of expedients—dangling tin pie plates, a scarecrow, my trusty Red Ryder BB gun coming to the rescue and plenty of yelling out the window—we usually managed to keep to birds away to a sufficient degree to obtain a good harvest. Pitting the result was a tedious process, but one of the end results I dearly loved was stewed cherries. Reaching the point of being ready to cook the cherries may have been demanding, but the actual preparation was the essence of simplicity.

*1 quart or ½ gallon sour cherries, pitted
Sugar to taste (figure at least 1 cup per
1 quart fruit)*

Place pitted cherries in a large pan or small stewpot; stir in sugar. Turn the burner to medium heat (to the point where the cherries are simmering) and stir constantly as the cherries cook. They should be ready to eat after 5 to 7 minutes of simmering.

—Jim Casada

❖ ❖ ❖

Chapter 17
FRUITS FROM THE WILD

T he fields and woodlands of Appalachia abound in fruits. Among the most widespread are persimmons and pawpaws, but wild plums, wild apricots, meat from honey locust pods and fruit from mulberry trees also merit consideration. These can be used in a wide variety of ways—fresh, in desserts, dried and canned or frozen for cooking weeks or months down the road.

Persimmon Bread

Persimmons grow wild across most of the southern Appalachians and, when fully ripe, form the basis of wonderful puddings. They are also delicious in sweet breads such as this offering.

3½ cups flour
1 teaspoon salt
2 teaspoons baking soda
Pinch (maybe ½ teaspoon) nutmeg or allspice
2 cups sugar
1 cup (2 sticks) butter, melted and cooled to room temperature
4 large eggs, lightly whisked
⅔ cup bourbon (a cheap brand is fine)

Comparing the sizes of an Oriental persimmon and a wild one. *Jim Casada.*

2 brimming cups persimmon pulp (fruits should be squishy ripe, and incidentally, pulp freezes well)
2 cups chopped and lightly toasted pecans or English walnuts
2 cups chopped dried fruit such as apricots, raisins, yellow raisins or dates

Preheat oven to 350. Butter a pair of loaf pans or use nonstick pans. Sift flour, salt, baking soda, spice and sugar into a large plastic mixing bowl. Whisk in the butter, eggs, bourbon and persimmon pulp until thoroughly mixed. Whisk in nuts and dried fruit. Place batter in pans and slide into preheated oven. Cooking time varies depending on the type of pan used. Check periodically as bread begins to brown by inserting a toothpick. When it comes out clean, the bread is ready.

NOTE: Once cooled, wrap to maintain moistness. The bread will keep several days (but likely be eaten much sooner), and it freezes well.

—Jim Casada

Persimmon Pudding

2 cups persimmon pulp (if you don't want the considerable work associated with readying wild ones, get the huge, seedless Oriental persimmons)
2 cups brown sugar, packed
¼ cup butter, melted
1 teaspoon vanilla
1 ½ cups self-rising flour
½ cup light cream or whole milk
2 eggs, beaten
½ teaspoon cinnamon
½ cup raisins or black walnuts (optional)

Combine all ingredients and beat just until well mixed. Pour into a greased 9" × 13" pan and bake at 350 degrees for 30 to 35 minutes

A group spreading a picnic during an outing at Heintooga. *Courtesy of Hunter Library, Western Carolina University.*

or until golden brown and just beginning to pull away from the sides. Remove from oven and cool slightly before cutting into squares. Serve with whipped cream.

NOTE: This is an exceptionally rich dish, and once you taste it, ready awareness of why persimmons are sometimes called "nature's candy" dawns.

—Jim Casada

Pawpaw Pudding

1 cup pawpaw pulp with all seeds removed
1 ¼ cups sugar
1 teaspoon baking powder
½ cup melted butter (the real thing)
1 teaspoon ginger (optional)
3 eggs
½ teaspoon salt

A cluster of pawpaws at harvesttime. *Jim Casada.*

1 teaspoon baking soda
2½ teaspoons cinnamon
½ teaspoon nutmeg

Strain the pawpaw pulp using a plastic sieve. Mix it with the rest of the ingredients and bake in a well-greased pan for approximately 1 hour at 350 degrees (when done, it will begin to pull away from the sides of the pan). Cool and cut into squares.

—Jim Casada

Chapter 18

MELONS

M elons have always drawn culinary raves, and who can resist the allure of an icy watermelon, so bursting with scarlet goodness that it splits asunder with the merest insertion of a butcher knife? Unquestionably, watermelons take pride of place in this foodstuff category, but other types of melons certainly have their place. There's even one widely grown "melon," historically popular through much of the region, that isn't even consumed. This is the Queen Anne's pocket melon or "plum granny," a miniature melon with an incredibly alluring aroma.

Among those offering tasty temptation to the Appalachian palate—in addition to old-time watermelons such as Georgia Cannonballs and Charleston Greys— are cantaloupes, honeydews and muskmelons (often called mushmelons). All are sweet, all contain considerable water and all are meant to be eaten fresh. You can freeze melon balls, but they require considerable space and don't come close to matching the fresh version. Melons can also be used creatively in drinks.

A watermelon on the vine growing toward delicious ripeness. *Tipper Pressley.*

WATERMELON WITH SALT

Tipper's Story

My parents, Pap and Granny, loved watermelon. Pap would bring one home and put it in the creek to cool. Then, of an evening, we'd take a knife, some towels and a saltshaker to the backyard to eat that sweet goodness. We'd spit seeds and talk while the stickiness ran down our arms. Sprinkling watermelon with salt really brightens the flavor.

Jim's Story

Grandpa Joe loved watermelon to an unbelievable degree, and many of my favorite summertime memories revolve around eating it with him. In early summer, he'd sometimes buy a melon, but the sandy soil in the lower portion of his sprawling garden situated alongside the Tuckaseigee River was perfect for their growth. Whether store-bought or home-grown, a watermelon cooled in a washtub where a chunk of ice taken from the icebox floated in the water was pure heaven. We'd have seed-spitting contests, and his free-range chickens loved those moments, scrambling to get every seed as soon as it touched the ground. The moisture of the melon and liberal sprinklings of salt replenished and refreshed "a body," as Grandpa put it, after hours of arduous work hoeing corn or performing some other garden chore.

Patriotic Melon Medley

Watermelons and honeydews ripen, at least in portions of the Appalachian South, in time for Independence Day celebrations. For an attractive color-themed offering at July Fourth celebrations, combine watermelon and honeydew balls with blueberries.

TIP: If you have trouble determining when a watermelon is ripe, there are a number of tricks to help you. If it hasn't been picked, the little tendrils on the vine where it attaches to the melon begin to turn yellow when the melon is ripe. For melons from the store, thumping and looking for yellow on the bottom (the brighter the yellow, the better)

A group enjoying a picnic. *Courtesy of Hunter Library, Western Carolina University.*

helps. But possibly the best test is using a broom straw, although some scoff at the approach. It involves balancing a broom straw atop a melon. If it rotates appreciably from the initial resting spot, the melon is deemed to be ripe.

—Jim Casada

Melon Balls with Country Ham

Fancy restaurants or hostesses offering lavish buffets often provide melon balls wrapped in thin slices of prosciutto. The meat is simply Italian ham that has been dry cured, and you'll find that substituting salt- or smoke-cured country ham for the prosciutto works in taste-tempting fashion. The saltiness of the ham blends perfectly with the sweetness of melon, and as is noted in the watermelon "recipe" (actually, in this case, more a guide to eating delight) that begins this chapter, many consider a hint of salt essential with melon.

Using a fillet knife or strong, sharp cheese slicer, cut slices of meat from a country ham. They should be so thin that light shines through

A pictorial tale of two seasons—a man with a halved watermelon stands on an iced-over Tuckaseigee River in downtown Bryson City, North Carolina. *Courtesy of Hunter Library, Western Carolina University.*

them. Cut to a size suitable for wrapping around a melon ball (or, alternatively, cut the melon in rectangular chunks). Hold the meat in place with a toothpick. Rest assured this will be a hit at picnics, family reunions and the like.

—Jim Casada

Chapter 19

BERRIES

HOMEGROWN AND FROM NATURE

A long with fruit, berries have enjoyed great appeal with the folks of Appalachia. For starters, they had a profusion of wild berries—strawberries, raspberries, dewberries, blackberries, elderberries, huckleberries, blueberries and others—available for the picking. All it took was gumption and a bucket. The former was in plentiful supply in a society where a staunch work ethic was almost a religion, while an old lard tin or a homemade birch bark receptacle served quite nicely as a container. Some folks included tame berry patches as an adjunct to gardens, as well—although this was not particularly common, with the exception of strawberries and, to a somewhat lesser degree, blueberries and raspberries. Today, that has changed dramatically, and home gardeners often raise a variety of berries, with thornless blackberries joining blueberries as being particularly popular. In yesteryear, gathering and canning berries was widely practiced, and berries contributed variety to the Appalachian diet when eaten fresh, prepared as a side dish or used in desserts. Here's a selection of recipes featuring them, and of course, they also hold a prominent place later in the book when matters turn to the sweet tooth.

A toddler all outfitted to pick berries. *Courtesy of Hunter Library, Western Carolina University.*

Blueberry Salad

2 cups blueberries
1 (6-ounce) package black cherry gelatin
1 cup water
1 (8½-ounce) can crushed pineapple, undrained
1 small carton whipped cream
1 (3-ounce) package cream cheese, softened
½ cup pecans, finely chopped

A blueberry bush laden with ripening berries. *Jim Casada.*

Place 1 cup of berries in a saucepan, cover with water and simmer until tender. Drain and reserve the juice. Add enough water to the blueberry juice to make 2 cups. Heat juice to boiling and add gelatin; stir until gelatin is dissolved. Add 1 cup cold water, pineapple, cooked blueberries and a cup of uncooked blueberries. Pour into a 9" x 13" dish and refrigerate until firm.

Beat softened cream cheese, add nuts and fold in whipped topping. Mix well. Spread over congealed salad and chill for at least 2 hours before serving.

—Jim Casada

Blackberry Dumplings

A blackberry dumpling adorned with ice cream. *Tipper Pressley.*

1 quart blackberries
1½ cups of sugar
Enough water to cover berries (more may be needed before adding dumplings)

Dumplings
1 cup self-rising flour
1 tablespoon sugar
½ cup milk

Place blackberries, sugar and water in saucepan and bring to a boil. Cook berries for about 20 minutes or until slightly thickened. More water may need to be added during cooking. Mix dumpling ingredients thoroughly and drop by tablespoons into boiling berries. Reduce heat. Cover and cook for 15 minutes or until dumplings are cooked through the center.

TIP: Serve hot with cream or ice cream.

—Tipper Pressley

Wild Strawberry/Spinach Salad

Freshly picked strawberries.
Tipper Pressley.

4 cups spinach, washed and torn
1 cup wild strawberries, hulled and washed (you can substitute tame ones)
1 kiwi, peeled and sliced (optional)
⅔ cup chopped macadamia nuts
2 tablespoons strawberry jam
2 tablespoons cider vinegar
⅓ cup oil

Combine spinach, strawberries, kiwi and nuts and set aside, then prepare dressing. Blend jam and vinegar, then add oil gradually as you continue to process. Use this to dress the salad.

—Jim Casada

Mulberry Juice Concentrate

Mulberries
Water
Sugar to taste

165

Wash mulberries and place in a large stockpot. Add water until you just begin to see it start coming up around the berries. Cook on medium low for 20 minutes or until juice is released from berries. Run mulberries through ricer or food mill to separate juice from berries. Discard pulp. Pour juice through fine sieve or cheesecloth to remove remaining seeds. Pour strained juice into clean saucepot, add sugar to taste and simmer for 10 minutes.

Mulberry juice may be kept in the refrigerator and used as wanted. Mix concentrate with water to serve.

—Tipper Pressley

Raspberry Trifle

Although wild raspberries are the essence of all that is delicious, and both red and black ones grow widely across southern Appalachia, you can substitute domestic ones.

2 cups raspberries
1 store-bought or homemade pound cake
1 tapioca or vanilla pudding made from dry mix
Whipped cream, homemade or from a squirt can

Cover the bottom of a large bowl (or trifle dish) with a layer of crumbled pound cake. Place a layer of raspberries over the cake, followed by a layer of vanilla or tapioca pudding and a layer of whipped cream. Repeat layers until bowl is full, ending with whipped topping dotted by fresh berries.

NOTE: This is a versatile recipe that also works well with other berries. If you particularly enjoy chocolate, substitute chocolate cake, chocolate pudding and crushed toffee pieces.

—Jim Casada

Chapter 20

DRIED FOODS

D rying was widely practiced by our forebears, and thanks to the modern availability of dehydrators, it is once more increasingly popular. Various types of foods—legumes, some fruits, berries and various vegetables—lend themselves to drying. The process intensifies taste and sometimes offers delightful differences in it. It requires little storage room, and most dried foods have a shelf life lasting from several months to years. Dried tomatoes, peppers, squash and okra can be added to soups and stews for flavor. Reconstituted squash, in particular, adds wonderful thickness. Also, peppers, both sweet and hot, can be dried and then pulverized to use just as you would ground black peppercorns (from a shaker, if you wish) to season foods. Tomatoes can likewise be ground into powder for a rich seasoning or to sprinkle atop salads.

On the fruit side, dried apples are often reconstituted and cooked as a sweet in Appalachia, but they are also used as a side dish mountain folks simply call *fruit* (as they also often describe canned apples). Dried apples are particularly savory when reconstituted and go wonderfully well with meals from breakfast to supper.

Gwendolyn and Mary Alice Bennett in the family garden. *Courtesy of Hunter Library, Western Carolina University.*

Soup Beans

Pinto beans
Water
Salt
Pepper
Seasoning: ham, hog jowl, fatback or bacon

Soup beans are one of the most common Appalachian foodstuffs. The humble pot of soup beans has literally kept the inhabitants of the Appalachian Mountains alive and well for generations. The first step in cooking soup beans is to look your beans: i.e., go through them carefully and discard any foreign materials such as rocks or leaves. After looking, rinse the beans a few times and then cover with water and allow to soak overnight.

Soup beans need to cook for many hours to become soft. A few different cooking options: cook beans on top of the stove, replenishing water as needed; cook soup beans in a slow cooker; or cook soup beans in a pressure cooker.

After you decide which method to use, you need to decide how to season the beans. Our favorite approach is to use fatback (salt pork), bacon or ham. Cover the beans with water, add seasoning and cook until done. When seasoning with salt and pepper to taste, keep in mind the salt content of the meat, if you're using a salt-cured option.

NOTE: In place of soaking beans overnight, boil looked beans for 2 minutes, remove the pot from heat and allow to sit for an hour before cooking.

TIP: Soup beans freeze well for later use.

—Tipper Pressley

Soup Beans and Ham Hock

2 cups dry beans
1 ham hock or soup bone
1 teaspoon black or red pepper

"Soup beans" always meant navy beans in the Casada family (for Tipper's, it was pintos—see previous recipe), but this recipe, the essence of simplicity, will work with any type of dried beans. In fact, my personal favorites are either pintos or October beans. No matter what kind of dried bean you start with, it is highly advisable to rinse them thoroughly in a colander as your first step. Any grit or dirt left from the harvesting process should be washed away. The next step is to put the beans in a large stewpot or soup pot and cover with water. Remove any beans that float immediately to the top or appear questionable in color.

Soaking can go in one of two directions. I usually cover the beans, with enough water to be 2 or 3 inches clear of the beans, and let them soak overnight. Rest assured they will soak up all the water and you'll likely need to add more when you're ready to cook. Alternatively, you can bring the dry beans to a rolling boil and then back off, letting the beans set for 20 to 30 minutes.

Either way, once you're ready to cook, add a ham hock (or soup bone, if you're lucky enough to have one left from a ham) and bring the pot to a boil before turning the heat down to a slow simmer. I like to add black pepper and a bit of red pepper at this point, although I hold off on any salt until the beans are tender and ready to serve. That's because the ham or ham hock will have considerable salt, and there's nothing more distressing than a big pot of soup beans that are too salty. Cook until thoroughly done and tender, but avoid overcooking and having the beans turn to mush. Serve with a big pone of cornbread and a fruit salad, and you are every bit as well off as folks eating fancy fixin's in four-star restaurants.

—Jim Casada

Gideon Laney
and his daughter,
Grace, cooking for
a Works Progress
Administration crew.
*Courtesy of Hunter
Library, Western
Carolina University.*

Spinach and Dried Tomatoes

Dried tomatoes, chopped or crumbled
Olive oil
Spinach
Salt and pepper to taste
Chickpeas (optional)

Soak tomatoes in hot water for 30 minutes. (If you are using dried tomatoes in oil, this step is not necessary.) Heat olive oil in pan, sauté spinach until it is almost done and add seasonings to taste. Add tomatoes and cook until warmed through. If using, add chickpeas. Adjust seasoning and serve. Makes a good side dish for any meal.

—Tipper Pressley

Split Pea Soup

1 cup ham, cooked and chopped
1 cup kielbasa or other link sausage, chopped
½ pound dried split green peas
2 carrots, chopped
2 potatoes, peeled and chopped
1 small onion, chopped
6 cups water
Salt and pepper to taste

In a large kettle, combine all ingredients and bring to a boil. Reduce heat and simmer covered 1 hour or until peas are tender. With a potato masher, mash vegetables right in kettle. Simmer uncovered about 15 minutes for a thick, hearty soup.

—Jim Casada

Black Bean Soup

2 cups black beans, cleaned, rinsed and soaked
1 ham hock
6 cups cold water
2 cups chicken broth
1 medium onion, chopped
1 garlic clove, minced
2 tablespoons margarine
2 bay leaves
2 tablespoons parsley

1 to 2 cups venison kielbasa or smoked venison sausage, finely chopped
Salt and pepper to taste
Cheddar cheese, shredded
Sour cream
Onion, chopped

Soak beans for at least 2 hours, then drain. Fill Dutch oven with ham hock, beans, water and broth. Cook on low until beans are tender. Sauté onion, garlic and parsley in margarine and add to soup along with bay leaves, parsley, kielbasa, salt and pepper. Continue cooking over low heat until beans are soft (about 3 hours). Add a small amount of water if the soup becomes too thick. Remove bay leaves and hock, chopping ham from the latter into small pieces and returning to the soup. Garnish with shredded cheddar cheese, sour cream and chopped onion.

—Jim Casada

Leather Britches

Leather britches have a totally different taste than fresh or canned green beans. The drying process gives them a deep rich, smoky flavor.

Leather britches (dried green beans)
Water
Salt and pepper to taste
Seasoning: fatback, bacon or ham

A pot of leather britches beans ready to cook. *Tipper Pressley.*

Soak leather britches overnight before cooking. Discard water and rinse. Add leather britches to pot and cover with water. Add salt and pepper to taste. Add your choice of meat to season the beans. My favorite meat to use is fatback (salt pork). For a mess of leather britches, I add two pieces of meat. Cook beans for several hours until soft. Additional water will need to be added, as the leather britches cook down over a long period of time. Since the leather britches are dried, they will take much longer to cook than fresh green beans.

TIP: Leather britches may be made from any type of green beans, but greasy beans and white half runners work especially well.

—Tipper Pressley

Crowder Peas

I've never known for sure what the "proper" name for these members of the legume family is. In the Casada family, we variously called them field peas, crowder peas and clay peas, and they go by other names, such as zip peas, purple hulls and pink eyes. They come in literally dozens of varieties, but all share a couple of things in common—they produce prolifically and are delicious to eat.

We normally shell and freeze 30 quarts or so, and our standard approach is to blanch them, put them in freezer bags and finish the cooking when they are ready to be eaten. I am partial to cooking them with streaked meat (anyone who grew up in the mountains will tell you that pork will dress up and improve the taste of most anything), but if you feel compelled to yield to the dictates of the weight and cholesterol nazis, just use a bit of low-sodium bouillon. Cook in a saucepan until done, and if you happen to be a fan of chowchow, as I am, top them with it. Otherwise, just enjoy them with cornbread and the rest of your victuals.

NOTE: Crowder peas are widely used as a menu item for New Year's Day. Supposedly, their brown color represents pennies.

—Jim Casada

Persimmon Leather

Hunters sometimes describe persimmons as "nature's candy" since deer are so drawn to this wild fruit, and there is no question about the sticky-sweet wonder of truly ripe ones. Persimmons contain appreciably less moisture than many fruits and lend themselves to drying. Gathering enough wild ones, removing their many seeds and obtaining sufficient pulp to make a pudding, much less persimmon leather, can be a chore. However, Oriental persimmons are easy to grow, bear early and carry fruit many times the size of their wild cousins while losing nothing when it comes to taste. They are ideal for persimmon leather.

The process is simple. Clean fully ripe Oriental persimmons when they are soft almost to the point of mushiness and mash them through a colander. That removes any fiber or hint of seeds while producing pulp ready for drying. Place in thin strips atop parchment paper in a dehydrator set at a fairly low temperature or on tinfoil in the sun. When dry, the leather will still be flexible, as opposed to brittle, and can be rolled up. It keeps best in a refrigerator or airtight jars; be aware that any vestiges of moisture can lead to mold. Leather can also be compacted and frozen. It makes a wonderful, chewy snack or can be reconstituted for persimmon pudding or bread.

—Jim Casada

Blueberry Upside Down Cake

My coauthor, Tipper, first brought this recipe to my attention. She uses fresh blueberries, but knowing that blueberries dry easily immediately suggested using dehydrated ones. Besides, like most avid cooks, I'm always intrigued by a bit of experimentation. In this case, it worked!

1 ½ sticks butter
½ cup brown sugar, packed
Reconstituted blueberries, enough to cover the bottom of a 9-inch cake pan or cast-iron pan
¾ cup sugar
2 large eggs (at room temperature)

2 teaspoons vanilla extract
1 cup all-purpose flour
1 teaspoon baking powder
Pinch salt
½ cup sour cream

Melt ⅓ of your butter (½ stick) in the cake pan. Stir in the brown sugar until it is fully blended. Add reconstituted blueberries to the pan bottom and distribute evenly for a full layer. Melt remaining butter and mix with sugar, eggs and vanilla using a whisk or beater. Add flour, baking powder and salt, stirring enough to combine. Add sour cream and whisk until combined (it helps to soften the sour cream by microwaving for a few seconds).

Pour batter over fruit and bake at 350 degrees for 45 minutes or until done. Remove from oven and cool for 5 to 10 minutes before turning onto a plate.

—Jim Casada

Chapter 21

PICKLES

n pre-electricity and pre-canning times, pickling, along with drying and
salting, represented an important way to preserve food. In much of the
Appalachians, it was made even more appealing thanks to the ready
availability of vinegar as a by-product of a popular and widespread crop,
apples. Almost any vegetable could be pickled and, for that matter, fruit
and meat as well. Over time and through tradition, certain types of pickles
became an integral and enjoyable part of regional diet. They gave zest to the
sameness or blandness of dried beans, offered cherished side dishes in forms
such as kraut and even figured on the sweet side through the likes of pickled
peaches and watermelon rind pickles. What follows is a bit of a cross section
of favorite southern Appalachian types of pickles.

Quick Pickled Ramps

1 pound ramps, cleaned
1 ½ cups white vinegar
1 ½ cups sugar
1 ½ cups water
¼ cup salt
1 tablespoon mustard seed
6 allspice berries

Two women with jugs and jars that probably hold apple cider or vinegar. *Courtesy of Hunter Library, Western Carolina University.*

Red pepper flakes to taste (at least a pinch)
1 bay leaf
Sterilized jars, lids and rings

Combine all ingredients except ramps. Bring to a rolling boil, stirring until sugar is dissolved. Pack ramps into jars and ladle brine over ramps to fill jars. Seal at once. After jars have cooled, store in refrigerator. Ramp pickles will be better after sitting for at least 4 weeks.

—Tipper Pressley

Pickled Peaches

During the summer months, my paternal grandmother, Grandma Minnie, always kept a jar of pickled peaches in her refrigerator. To come in the house and eat one of those peaches after a hot session of hard, honest work hoeing out corn or something less productive but equally tiring—such as knocking down a wasp's nest so Grandpa Joe and I could get some prime fishing bait—was pure pleasure.

1 vitamin C tablet, crushed—or similar acidulation agent (such as Fruit Fresh)
Cold water (enough to cover fruit)
2 dozen small peaches, peeled (early clingstones do particularly well)
2½ cups sugar
1¼ cups distilled white vinegar
4 teaspoons pickling spice
1 tablespoon whole cloves
Pinch salt

Put water with dissolved acidulation agent—to prevent discoloration—in a large bowl. Place peaches in the water and allow to stand for 10 minutes, stirring a couple of times during this period. Drain well using a colander and then toss with the sugar. Chill for 10 to 12 hours in a large covered pot or the bowl used for acidulation covered with a wrap, such as an old towel or cheesecloth.

Jars of pickled peaches.
Tipper Pressley.

Add vinegar, spice, salt and ½ cup water to chilled peaches and bring to a boil. Skim off the foam, reduce heat and simmer for a few minutes until peaches are tender. Place peaches in sterilized canning jars that have been sitting in hot water, making sure to get 1 or 2 whole cloves in each jar. Bring reserved liquid from the peaches to a boil and pour over peaches. Run an ice pick or thin knife between peaches to remove any air bubbles. Close jars with canning lids and screw tops and process for 20 to 25 minutes in a water-bath canner (not a pressure cooker) before removing and allowing to seal.

—Jim Casada

Squash and Zucchini Pickles

4 quarts squash or zucchini or a mixture of both, sliced
2 quarts sliced onions
½ cup salt
2 quarts ice
5 cups sugar (may be reduced to 3 cups for a less sweet pickle)
5 cups vinegar
1 ½ teaspoons turmeric
1 teaspoon celery seed
2 teaspoons mustard seed
Sterilized jars, lids and rings

Mix squash, onions and salt. Cover with ice and let sit for three hours. Drain squash mixture and set aside. Combine all other ingredients and heat just to boiling. Add drained squash mixture and heat for about 5 minutes. Ladle hot pickles and liquid into clean jars and seal. Process in a water-bath canner for 5 minutes. After cooling, make sure all jars have sealed before storing for future use.

—Tipper Pressley

Bread and Butter Pickles

4 quarts cucumbers (or combination of squash, zucchini and cucumbers)
6 onions, diced
½ hot pepper, diced
1 quart sweet peppers
3 cloves garlic, minced
⅓ cup non-iodized salt
1½ teaspoons turmeric
5 cups sugar
1½ teaspoons celery seed
2 tablespoons mustard seed
3 cups apple cider vinegar

Combine vegetables and garlic in large bowl. Mix salt and turmeric and stir into bowl. Cover bowl and allow to sit for 3 hours. The smell of the pickles at this stage will starve you to death!

After 3 hours, drain pickles and place in large pot. Combine sugar, celery seed, mustard seed and apple cider vinegar. Pour over cucumber mixture and heat until boiling. While pickles are still hot, pack into sterilized jars, leaving ½-inch headspace; add lids and rings. Process in a water-bath canner for 10 minutes.

—Tipper Pressley

Pickled Okra

3 pounds okra pods, washed
6 hot or mild red or green peppers (a mixture works well)
6 cloves garlic
1 quart white vinegar
1⅓ cups water
½ cup salt
1 tablespoon mustard seed
Sterilized pint jars, lids and rings

Trim stems, but do not cut into pods. Pack okra into clean jars; add peppers and garlic to each jar. Combine remaining ingredients and bring to a boil. Pour liquid over okra, leaving ½-inch headspace. Seal and process in boiling-water canner for 10 minutes. Makes 6 pints.

—Tipper Pressley

Kraut

Shredded cabbage
Non-iodized salt
A few large cabbage leaves
Crock or large glass container

For every 8 to 10 cups of cabbage, you need 1 tablespoon of salt. Begin layering cabbage and salt in container, massaging the cabbage as you go. This will allow the cabbage to start releasing liquid. Continue this process until you run out of cabbage or are within three inches of the container top. The cabbage needs to be submerged beneath the brine. If cabbage doesn't produce enough liquid, a brine of 2 teaspoons of salt to 1 cup of water can be used.

Press cabbage leaves on top of kraut to ensure cabbage remains submerged. A small saucer, a plate topped by a canning jar full of water or a plastic bag filled with water and tightly sealed can be used as a weight to press down the leaves. Cover container with a towel and secure with string. Place in a cool, dry place to allow kraut to work off. Begin checking kraut after two weeks to see if it is sour enough for your preferences. If not, allow kraut to continue to work another week or more.

Once kraut has finished working, it can be canned or stored in the refrigerator for future eating. In the old days, folks left kraut in the crock and dipped it out as needed.

NOTES:

1. A small amount of mold on top of working kraut is normal. If the batch truly goes bad, you will know right away from the horrid smell.
2. Many, if not most, folks experienced with making kraut swear by

following the astrological signs when making kraut, just as many adhere to them when planting crops while others believe they guide daily life. Each zodiac sign equates to a body part. Signs above the waist are deemed best for kraut, with the head sign being especially desirable.

—Tipper Pressley

Pickled Corn

Fresh corn sliced from cobs
Water
Non-iodized salt

Boil corn for 3 minutes. Allow to cool in cold water and slice from cob. Add 2 teaspoons of non-iodized salt to a sterilized canning jar; fill with corn. Pour warm water over corn, leaving ¼-inch headspace. Seal jars loosely so corn can work, and place atop a tray to catch any liquid that escapes. Allow to sit for 14 days in a cool dry place. May be stored in refrigerator for future use.

—Tipper Pressley

Watermelon Rind Pickles

While most recipes call for cutting away the outer peeling and removing any red flesh next to the rind, my Grandma Minnie left the rind intact as well as a bit of the melon next to it. It gave her pickles an attractive color and variety in texture.

Watermelon rinds
4 tablespoons salt
1 quart water

Pickle Syrup
8 cups sugar
4 cups vinegar

8 teaspoons whole cloves
12 cinnamon sticks
Pinch mustard seed (optional)

Cut the watermelon rind into 1-inch cubes and allow to soak in the brine overnight. The next morning, drain off the liquid, add fresh water and cook the rinds until tender.

Then prepare the pickle syrup, boiling the mixture and then allowing it to sit for 15 minutes. Add drained watermelon rind and cook until the cubes become somewhat transparent. Process in sterilized jars. Properly done, this sweet pickle will be crunchy, tasty and appealing to the eye.

—Jim Casada

Chowchow

A relish that belongs to a bowl of October beans the way red-eye gravy partners cured ham, chowchow is an old-time Appalachian favorite. It offered mountain folks a way of preserving a wide variety of vegetables through what was, in essence, a pickling process. Other than the common denominators of cabbage and vinegar, the variations on chowchow contents are almost endless. Here's a pretty standard approach.

2 heads cabbage, diced fairly fine
6 large green tomatoes, diced
4 tablespoons pickling salt
4 pods dried red pepper, crushed (amount can vary according to
your heat preferences)
1 cup water
4 or 5 cups white vinegar

Place the vegetables in a large stoneware crock and then add the other ingredients. Mix thoroughly and pack tightly, being sure the liquid (brine) rises over the top. Cover with cheesecloth and let set in a warm room until the chowchow "works." Store in pint or quart jars.

—Jim Casada

Chapter 22
JELLIES, JAMS AND FRUIT BUTTERS

As an adornment for cathead biscuits, filling for some types of layer cakes or topping for pancakes, or used in a variety of other fashions, what Appalachian folks typically describe with the generic, catchall word *preserves* has long been of culinary significance. The "preserve" part is critical, because the recipes that follow offer a cross section of ways to utilize the goodness of fruits and berries long after their short season of ripe, fresh availability has come and gone. It is also worth mentioning some of the tools of the jam- and jelly-making trade that come in handy. A fine sieve works well to remove seeds. It is common for foam to form on top as the jelly juice boils; it can be skimmed off with a homemade wooden skimmer somewhat similar to those you find in paint stores (just be sure the wood you use is suitable). Alternatively, adding a teaspoon of butter at the outset of cooking helps decrease foam.

Blackberry Jelly
Blackberry jelly is one of the easiest things to make. The only hard part takes place before you ever start cooking. First, you have to fight the heat, bugs, snakes, bees and briars to pick the blackberries. It takes about 2½ quarts of blackberries to get the amount of juice needed for a run of jelly.

2½ quarts of blackberries (yield is about 3¾ cups blackberry juice)
1 (1¾-ounce) box powdered fruit pectin
4½ cups sugar
Sterilized jars, lids and rings

Place blackberries in a large stockpot and add water until you can just begin to see it come up around the berries. Cook for 20 minutes. Mash berries every once in a while during cooking with a potato masher or spoon.

Strain blackberries, reserving juice to make jelly and discarding cooked blackberries (chickens and hogs will welcome the pulp being thrown away).

A handful of blackberries ready to be worked up. *Tipper Pressley.*

I use a food mill to do my first straining of the blackberries and then use cheesecloth to filter out the seeds that made their way into the juice. Place blackberry juice into a large saucepot, add pectin and stir well. Bring mixture to a boil. I'm not sure there's anything that smells as good as blackberry juice when it's cooking. Add sugar all at once and stir to combine. Bring mixture back to a full rolling boil and boil 1 minute.

Quickly ladle hot liquid into sterilized jars and seal.

NOTE: If you have enough blackberry juice, this recipe is easily doubled. If you don't have quite enough for a second run, you can freeze what you have until you harvest more blackberries for juice.

—Tipper Pressley

Mulberry Jelly

4 quarts mulberries
1 cup water
1 (1¾-ounce) box powdered fruit pectin
3 tablespoons lemon juice
5 cup sugar

After washing mulberries, put them in a large saucepot with water. Cook on medium heat until berries begin to simmer, then cook 10 minutes more. Use back of spoon or potato masher to mash mulberries every once in a while to encourage them to release their juice. Drain mulberries, reserving juice to make jelly and discarding cooked mulberries. I use a food mill to do my first straining of the mulberries and then I use cheesecloth to filter out the seeds that made their way into the juice. I do the same thing when I make blackberry jelly (see previous recipe). I don't like seeds. Pour strained juice into a large saucepot and stir in the box of pectin and the lemon juice. Heat juice until it comes to a full rolling boil then add sugar. Stir sugar until it's combined well with juice. Allow juice to come to another boil, then boil for 1 minute. Quickly ladle hot liquid into sterilized jars and seal.

TIP: I do not remove the mulberry stems, and the jelly still turns out great.

—Tipper Pressley

Fox Grape Jelly

In my family, at least—and my study of regional cookbooks suggests this is generally the case in the South—there was a pretty simple, straightforward method for making fox grape jelly. One of its advantages was that there's enough natural pectin in fox grapes to make the jelly set nicely without using anything beyond fruit and sugar.

Clusters of fox grapes hold promise of tasty treats come early autumn.
Tipper Pressley.

8 to 10 quarts fox grapes
¾ cup sugar for each cup pulp/juice mixture

Start by squeezing the pulp from the skins and placing in separate bowls. Remove the seeds from the pulp. This is easily done using a plastic sieve with small holes. Discard the seeds. Cook the skins until they are tender, strain and then combine with the pulp/juice mix that you have once the seeds have been removed. For each cup of the recombined mixture, add ¾ cup of sugar or to taste (some folks like fox grape jelly with a bit of tart bite to it). Bring the mixture to a slow boil for 10 to 20 minutes, stirring frequently until it becomes noticeably thick. At this point, pour into half-pint or pint jars and allow to cool. Seal with melted paraffin or two-piece lids. A cup of fruit with the seeds removed will make about ½ pint of jelly.

—Jim Casada

Grape Jelly

5 cups grape juice
1 (1¾-ounce) box powdered fruit pectin
7 cups sugar

Pour juice into a large saucepot and stir in pectin. Cook over medium-high heat and bring mixture to a full rolling boil. Add sugar all at once and stir. When juice returns to a full rolling boil, boil for 1 minute. Immediately ladle hot jelly into sterilized hot jars and seal.

—Tipper Pressley

Peach Jelly

4 cups peach juice, from peach skins and salvaged flesh from fruit
that is going bad
½ teaspoon butter (optional)
1 (1¾-ounce) box powdered fruit pectin
5½ cups sugar
Sterilized jars, lids and rings

Place peach skins and flesh in pot and cover with water. Bring to a boil. Once mixture is boiling, turn down to medium/low and let simmer for 10 minutes. Let mixture cool slightly. Strain juice. If you have less than

4 cups of juice, you can add water to make up the difference, but don't use more than 1 cup of water. If you have more than 4 cups of juice, you can double the recipe or freeze extra for later use. Place juice, butter and pectin in a pot on high heat and bring to a boil. Add sugar all at once and stir well. Bring mixture to a full rolling boil and boil for 1 minute. Ladle jelly into hot jars and seal.

NOTE: Peach pits are said to be poisonous; however, one would have to ingest a whole lot of ground-up peach seeds to be poisoned. Peach seeds can be left out if so desired.

—Tipper Pressley

Old-Fashioned Pear Preserves

Many folks have fond memories of the pear preserves their mother or grandmother made every year from cooking pears. At least four generations of my family have used this simple yet delicious recipe for pear preserves.

1 peck or more of cooking pears, cored and sliced
1½ cups sugar for every 2 quarts prepared pears

Old-fashioned pear preserves made from "cooking" pears. *Tipper Pressley.*

Peel pears and slice into slivers as big or small as you like. Place the sliced pears in a bowl, pour the sugar over them, stir, cover and allow to sit overnight in the refrigerator. The pears will make a little juice overnight. The amount of juice will depend on how ripe your pears are. If the pears don't produce sufficient juice overnight (enough to make a slurry or keep them from scorching over medium low heat), additional water can be added.

After removing the pears from the refrigerator, cook on medium low in a large pot for 15 minutes. Ladle hot pears into sterilized jars and seal. Process 10 minutes in a boiling-water canner.

TIP: I've used several varieties of pears, and the recipe always turns out well, but it is an especially useful way of dealing with hard or "cooking" pears.

—Tipper Pressley

Easy Persimmon Butter

Wash persimmons thoroughly and remove stems and other debris. Drain well. Press through a non-aluminum sieve to remove skins and seeds. Add a bit of honey (to taste) and mix well with a fork. Store in refrigerator and use as a spread on bagels, biscuits, muffins or toast.

NOTE: Persimmon pulp freezes well, and whenever you have a craving for its distinctive taste, a portion of the fruit can be thawed and converted to butter.

—Jim Casada

Chapter 23
CAKES

Some dessert recipes have long been standards in Appalachia—favorites for the holidays, "must take" items for family reunions or dinner-on-the-grounds gatherings or favorite family sweets sure to be served on almost any special occasion. Here's a sampling of these, from perhaps the best known of all Appalachian desserts, stack cake (the second recipe in this chapter), to various family favorites. Note that apples, appropriately, figure quite prominently in the coverage.

Raw Apple Cake

1 ¾ cups sugar
3 eggs
½ teaspoon salt
1 teaspoon cinnamon
1 cup oil
2 cups all-purpose flour
1 teaspoon baking soda
1 teaspoon vanilla
5 apples, sliced thin or diced
1 cup chopped pecans (divided in half)

Combine all ingredients, except apples and nuts, until well blended. Add apples and ½ cup of pecans and mix well. Pour batter into a greased 9" × 13" pan and sprinkle remaining nuts on top of batter. Bake at 350 degrees for 40 to 45 minutes or until done.

—Tipper Pressley

Apple Stack Cake

Part 1: Cake
½ cup sugar
½ cup shortening
1 egg, beaten
⅓ cup sorghum syrup
1 teaspoon vanilla
½ cup buttermilk
3½ cups all-purpose flour
½ teaspoon baking soda
½ teaspoon salt
1 teaspoon ginger

Cream together sugar and shortening. Add egg, sorghum, vanilla and buttermilk; mix well. Sift together flour, baking soda, salt and ginger. Make a hole in the dry ingredients, add the creamed mixture and stir until the consistency is like soft cookie dough.

The next step is making the cake layers. Divide dough into seven equal parts. You'll need to add additional flour as you roll out the dough to make the layers. Roll each layer into a 9-inch circle. Bake layers at 350 degrees for 10 to 12 minutes or until light brown around the edges. Set cooked layers aside to cool.

Part 2: Apple Filling
1 pound (14 cups) dried apples
Water
1 cup brown sugar
½ cup white sugar

A traditional apple stack cake dusted with powdered sugar and nicely decorated. *Tipper Pressley.*

1 teaspoon cinnamon
¼ teaspoon cloves
½ teaspoon allspice

Put apples in a pot with sufficient water to cover and cook; keep a fairly close eye on the apples, as you may have to add additional water while they cook. Once apples are soft enough to mash, add the other ingredients and mix well.

Part 3: Assembly

Place one cake layer on a cake plate and spread with apple filling. Repeat until you reach the last layer. Whether you put apple filling on the top layer is up to you. Many cooks use cooked apples to frost the entire cake. I like to leave the top layer bare and sprinkle powdered sugar on it in a pretty shape. This should not be done until just before serving; otherwise, the powdered sugar will just soak in and not provide the lovely dusted appearance.

Allow cake to sit overnight before eating. This enables the apple goodness to soak fully into the cake layers.

Part 4: Custard Sauce
4 egg yolks
½ cup sugar
2 cups half-and-half
1 teaspoon vanilla
Pinch salt

Custard sauce is not part of the traditional apple stack cake recipe; however, in my opinion, it makes a good thing an even better thing.

To make the sauce: Beat yolks in a metal bowl that will fit atop a saucepan in the manner of a double boiler. As you beat the yolks, add sugar a little at a time. Once sugar is added, increase the mixer speed, scraping bowl as needed, and beat until mixture is thick and lemon colored. Add half-and-half; mix well. Place bowl atop saucepan of simmering water. Cook custard over water, stirring often until mixture is thick enough to coat the back of a spoon. Add vanilla and salt. Remove from heat and cool before serving. This is a thin custard, which makes it perfect for pouring over a piece of cake.

Part 5: Eat
After the apple stack cake has sat overnight, slice a piece and drizzle custard over it or under it—or don't drizzle custard over it or under it at all—and eat!

NOTE: If you end up with more layers or less, the cake will still be amazingly good!

Also, while dried apples form the traditional filling between layers in stack cakes, various jams or reconstituted dried peaches will also work perfectly well.

TIP: Use the bottom of a 9-inch cake pan as a template for making cake layers by either tracing out the shape on parchment paper and rolling to size or rolling out dough and using the cake pan as a template to cut the dough out.

—Tipper Pressley

Arsh Tater Cake

Irish potato, noun—(a) variant forms arsh potato, arsh tater; (b) the common white potato with Irish added to distinguish it from a sweet potato. —Dictionary of Smoky Mountain English

This is my favorite traditional Appalachian dessert.

Cake
3 egg whites
2 cups all-purpose flour
2 teaspoons baking powder
1 teaspoon baking soda
¼ teaspoon salt
½ cup butter, softened
2 cups sugar
1 teaspoon cocoa
1 teaspoon vanilla
1 cup mashed potatoes, warm (can be leftover from a meal)
½ cup milk
1 cup black walnuts

Icing
1 cup sweet cream or evaporated milk
1 cup sugar
3 egg yolks, beaten
1 lump (1 tablespoon) butter
1 ½ cups shredded sweetened coconut
1 cup black walnuts

An arsh potato cake dripping with goodness. *Tipper Pressley.*

To make the cake, beat egg whites until light and fluffy; set aside. Sift together flour, baking powder, baking soda and salt and set aside. Cream butter and sugar. Add cocoa and vanilla; mix well. Add mashed potatoes; mix well. Alternately add dry ingredients and milk; mix well after each addition. Fold in black walnuts and egg whites. Pour batter into greased and floured 9-inch cake pans. Using parchment-lined pans helps prevent sticking. Bake at 350 degrees for 30 minutes or until done. Insert a toothpick to check; when it comes away dry, the cake is ready. Remove cake from pans and let cool.

To make the icing, cook cream, sugar and reserved egg yolks over low heat until thick; remove from heat. Stir in butter, coconut and black walnuts.

To assemble, place one cake layer on a cake stand; pour half of the icing on top; place the other layer on top and add the rest of the icing, spreading it evenly and allowing it to drip down the sides.

—Tipper Pressley

❖ ❖ ❖

Strawberry Shortcake

A serving of strawberry shortcake. *Tipper Pressley.*

1 quart strawberries, sliced
½ cup sugar
2 cups all-purpose flour
1 tablespoon plus 1 teaspoon baking powder
¼ teaspoon salt
¼ cup sugar
½ cup butter, cut into small pieces
½ cup milk
2 large eggs, separated
¼ cup sugar
Whipped cream or whipped topping

Sprinkle sliced strawberries with ½ cup sugar, stir, cover and chill while preparing the cake.

To make the cake, combine flour, baking powder, salt and ¼ cup sugar. Cut butter into flour mixture until mixture is crumbly. Combine milk and egg yolks, beat well and then add to flour mixture and mix with a fork until a soft dough forms. Divide dough in half. Press each half into a greased 9-inch cake pan. This dough is sticky; wetting your fingers makes it easier to pat down.

Beat reserved egg whites until stiff. Divide egg whites in half and gently spread over each dough layer. Sprinkle egg whites with ¼ cup sugar. Bake at 450 degrees for 8 minutes or until golden brown. Allow cakes to cool on wire rack.

While cake is baking, whip up some homemade whipping cream or get your store-bought whipped cream ready to use. If you'd like to serve the entire cake at a meal, place one cake layer on a serving plate, spread half of the whipped cream over the layer and arrange half of the sliced strawberries on top. Repeat with the other layer. Alternately, whipped cream and strawberries may be added to each piece as it's served to prevent sogginess.

Adding the beaten egg whites sprinkled with sugar to the top of the dough really gives this cake a nice crunch that contrasts with the soft berries and creamy topping.

—Tipper Pressley

Apple-Nut Cake

Cake
3 cups all-purpose flour
1 teaspoon baking soda
1 teaspoon salt
2 cups sugar
1 ½ cups cooking oil
3 eggs
2 teaspoons vanilla
3 cups finely diced apples
½ cup chopped pecans or English walnuts

Combine flour, baking soda, salt, sugar and oil; mix well. Add eggs one at a time, beating after each. Add vanilla, apples and nuts. Pour into a 9" × 13" baking pan. Bake at 325 degrees for 1 hour or until done (check with a toothpick at the hour mark). It takes only an hour in my oven. Pour glaze on while cake is still hot.

Glaze
1 stick butter
1 cup evaporated milk
1 cup brown sugar

Combine all ingredients in a small saucepan; bring to a boil and boil for 2 to 3 minutes. Pour over hot cake.

—Tipper Pressley

Summer Upside Down Cake

¾ cup butter, divided
½ cup brown sugar, packed
Your favorite fruit, enough to cover bottom of 9-inch cake pan or cast-iron pan
1 cup sugar
2 large eggs, at room temperature
2 teaspoons vanilla
1 cup all-purpose flour
1 teaspoon baking powder
½ teaspoon salt
½ cup sour cream

Melt ¼ cup butter in a pan and stir in brown sugar. Swirl pan around to make sure the mixture spreads evenly. Add fruit to bottom of pan. Melt remaining butter and mix with sugar, eggs and vanilla. Beat on high for 2 minutes. Add flour, baking powder and salt, mixing until just combined. Add sour cream and mix until combined. Pour batter over fruit and bake at 350 degrees for 45 minutes or until done. Cool for 5 minutes and then turn out on serving plate or cake stand. A very impressive-looking dessert.

TIP: You can use reconstituted dried blueberries in this recipe.

—Tipper Pressley

Fresh Apple Cake

Cake
4 eggs
3 cups sugar
3 cups self-rising flour

1 cup raisins
1 cup cooking oil
3 cups diced apples
1 cup black walnuts
2 teaspoons vanilla

Beat the eggs and then add remaining ingredients. Batter will be stiff. Bake in a 9" × 13" cake pan for 1 hour at 350 degrees.

Frosting

1 (13-ounce) package cream cheese
¼ cup butter or margarine
2 cups powdered sugar
1 teaspoon vanilla

Blend frosting ingredients with a mixer, a pulser or by hand. Allow cake to cool before applying the frosting.

—Jim Casada

Applesauce Cake

This is a traditional Christmas dessert in the mountain regions of the South.

My mother often prepared applesauce cakes over the Thanksgiving weekend for use at Yuletide. The ensuing weeks would see cakes stored in a cool area and periodically anointed with a few tablespoons of apple cider or wine to keep them moist. This combination of aging and moisturizing produced a cake that was, by the time Christmas rolled around and it was sliced, soaked through and through with toothsome goodness. It was so moist that the slices literally glistened.

Black walnuts hanging on the limb.
Tipper Pressley.

1 cup butter
2 cups sugar
3 cups applesauce

4 cups flour
⅓ cup cocoa
4 teaspoons baking soda
1 teaspoon cinnamon
2 teaspoons allspice
2 cups raisins
2 cups black walnut meats
2 teaspoons vanilla
Pinch salt

Cream butter and sugar. Add applesauce and remaining ingredients a small amount at a time, stirring by hand as you do so. Bake in a 10-inch tube pan for 50 minutes to an hour at 350 degrees. Check with toothpick to see if cake is done; if so, it will come away clean.

—Jim Casada

Black Walnut Pound Cake
This recipe came from the late Beulah Suddereth, as good a soul and fine a cook as ever called Swain County home, not to mention being a treasured family friend. I was blessed to have known her well.

Cake
1 cup butter (no substitute)
½ cup shortening
3 cups sugar
6 eggs
3 cups all-purpose flour, sifted
1 teaspoon baking powder
1½ cups finely chopped black walnuts
1 teaspoon vanilla
1 cup half-and-half

OPTIONAL: For a moister cake, add 8 ounces of sour cream.

Cream butter and shortening thoroughly. Gradually add sugar; cream until light and fluffy. Add eggs one at a time, beating well after each.

Slices of black walnut pound cake. *Corie Graddick.*

In a separate bowl, sift flour and baking powder and add chopped black walnuts. In a measuring cup, add vanilla to half-and-half. Add flour and walnut mixture and half-and-half alternately to creamed mixture, and if you opt to use sour cream, alternate it as well. Blend and mix well (beating well is the secret to a fine pound cake). Pour into a prepared 10-inch tube pan. Bake at 325 degrees for 1 hour and 15 minutes or until done. Cool for 10 minutes and remove from pan. You can, if desired, prepare a frosting for this cake.

Black Walnut Frosting
1 stick butter, melted
1 (16-ounce) box powdered sugar
Half-and-half or whole milk
¼ to ½ cup finely chopped black walnuts

Blend melted butter and powdered sugar. Add enough half-and-half to reach desired consistency. Fold in walnuts and frost cooled cake (do not put frosting atop cake until it is fully cooled).

—Jim Casada

Strawberry Punch Bowl Cake

1 quart strawberries
Sugar to taste
1 (16-ounce) box powdered sugar
1 small (5-ounce) can evaporated milk
1 (8-ounce) container whipped topping
1 (16-ounce) container sour cream
1 large angel food or sponge cake, cut or broken into small cubes

Slice or chop strawberries and mix with sugar. Set aside. The longer you let your strawberries set, the juicier they will be.

Mix powdered sugar, evaporated milk, whipped topping and sour cream together until smooth. Layer cake, strawberries and powdered sugar mixture in a bowl, ending with strawberries on top.

After assembling cake, allow to sit in refrigerator for several hours or overnight to let the strawberries and cream mixture soak into the cake pieces.

While strawberries are my favorite fruit to use in this recipe, peaches and blueberries are also very tasty.

NOTE: Adding whole strawberries as the top layer makes an especially pretty presentation.

TIP: If you have a clear punch bowl, this cake looks really pretty in it, but if you don't, just use a large bowl—the cake will still be just as good.

—Tipper Pressley

Chapter 24

PIES AND COBBLERS

T hanks to their being comparatively easy to make and to the ready availability of key ingredients in season, pies and cobblers have long held sway as standards of the sweet portion of daily diet in Appalachia. Of course, mere mention of the word *sweet* also conjures up thoughts of cakes, jams, jellies, syrups, honey and the like, but those are covered elsewhere. This chapter offers a cross section of pies and cobblers, and as a general rule, it should be noted that substituting one fruit or berry for another is perfectly feasible in many of the recipes that follow.

Grandma Minnie's Fried Pies

1 pound dried fruit
¾ cup brown sugar
2 teaspoons cinnamon (or to taste)
2 tablespoons butter
1 pie crust
Lard for frying
Cinnamon or cinnamon sugar

Cover the dried fruit with water and soak overnight. Drain any extra water and cook slowly until completely tender. Mash the fruit to make a sauce and then add the other ingredients. Stir well and allow to cool.

Make a pie crust, but use less shortening than normal. Roll out the crust quite thin, cut in circles (using a saucer for an outline provides a convenient size), add fruit sauce to each circle, fold over and pinch edges to seal. The end result is often called mule ears or half-moons because of their shape. Fry in piping hot lard; turn only once. Serve while still warm. If desired, you can sprinkle with cinnamon or cinnamon sugar.

TIP: Fried pies warm over quite nicely, and they also make a wonderful cold dessert for a field lunch.

—Jim Casada

Plum and Honey Tarts

1 sheet frozen puff pastry
Plums, sliced
Sugar
Honey

A tempting trio of plum tarts.
Tipper Pressley.

Thaw pastry according to directions (or if you wish, make your own). Using a sharp knife or an ulu, cut pastry into two-inch squares and place on greased or parchment-lined baking sheet. Prick pastry with a fork to prevent it from puffing up too much while cooking. Lay plum slices on pastry, leaving a slight border of perhaps ¼ inch around the edges. Sprinkle lightly with sugar and bake at 425 degrees for 25 minutes or until golden brown. Drizzle with honey just before serving.

TIP: Peaches and pears also work nicely with this simple recipe.

—Tipper Pressley

Beehives. *Courtesy of the National Park Service.*

Blackberry Pie

6 cups blackberries
1 cup sugar
½ cup water
¼ cup cornstarch
2 tablespoons fresh lemon juice
2 tablespoons butter
1 baked pie shell

Cook 2 cups of blackberries with sugar, water, cornstarch, lemon juice and butter. Bring to a simmer and cook for 1 minute until mixture has thickened. Place 2 cups of blackberries on the bottom of the pie shell. Pour cooked mixture over them and add the remaining 2 cups of blackberries to the top. Chill for 4 hours. Makes a very pretty summertime pie.

—Tipper Pressley

Peach Pie

2 unbaked pie crusts
4 cups sliced peaches
2 heaping tablespoons all-purpose flour
1 cup plus 1 tablespoon sugar
½ stick butter
1 egg white

Press one pie crust into pie plate. Add peaches and sprinkle with flour and 1 cup of sugar. Cut butter into pieces and add to top of peaches. Put the second crust on top, crimping the edges together with the bottom crust. Brush top with egg white and sprinkle the additional tablespoon of sugar on it. With a sharp knife, cut lines in the center of the top crust to allow steam to escape. Bake at 350 degrees for 1 hour or until crust is golden brown.

After the pie is removed from the oven, allow to cool for 30 minutes if you want the juices to set. We usually cut it as soon as it comes out of the oven because sweet, drippy juice doesn't bother us at all. Moreover, the aroma is of the "I can't wait" nature.

TIP: Place a baking sheet under the pie plate in oven to catch any drips.

—Tipper Pressley

Aunt Mary Jo's Apple Pie

2 cups diced apples
2 tablespoons water
1 unbaked pie shell
½ stick butter
¾ cup sugar
1 tablespoon all-purpose flour
1 teaspoon cinnamon
½ teaspoon salt
1 egg, slightly beaten

Place apples in a small saucepot with 2 tablespoons of water. Cook covered for 5 minutes with lid on, keeping an eye on it to make sure the apples don't scorch. Pour cooked apples with liquid into an unbaked pie shell. Melt butter in a small pot; remove from heat; stir in sugar, flour, cinnamon, salt and egg. Pour mixture over apples. Bake in a 350-degree oven for 35 minutes or until golden brown.

TIP: Store-bought pie shells work perfectly well, but if you are a real traditionalist and want the ultimate in both freshness and taste, make your own.

—Tipper Pressley

Peach Cobbler

½ cup butter
1 cup all-purpose flour
1 cup sugar
1 cup whole milk
2 cups sliced, cooked peaches

Place butter in a 9" × 13" baking dish and place in cold oven. Preheat oven to 350 degrees and allow butter to melt in pan as oven heats up. Combine flour, sugar and milk. Once butter has melted, remove pan, pour the butter in the batter and gently mix. Pour the batter into the heated pan and spoon peaches on top of it. Do not stir. Bake for 30 to 40 minutes or until golden brown on top.

A serving of peach cobbler. *Tipper Pressley.*

TIP: If you're using fresh peaches, cook peaches with one cup of water and ½ cup sugar for 25 to 30 minutes before starting this recipe.

—Tipper Pressley

Blackberry Cobbler

1 quart blackberries
½ cup water
1½ cups sugar, divided
1 teaspoon lemon juice (optional)
1 cup self-rising flour
1 cup buttermilk
½ teaspoon cinnamon
¼ cup butter
Dash of salt

Melt butter in 9" × 13" pan. In saucepot, combine blackberries, water and ½ cup sugar. Cook until mixture is hot and sugar is dissolved.

Remove from heat and add lemon juice. Combine 1 cup sugar and flour in a bowl. Stir in buttermilk and cinnamon. Pour batter over melted butter; do not stir. Spoon berries over the batter; do not stir. Bake at 350 degrees for 30 to 35 minutes or until top is golden brown.

TIP: If using all-purpose flour, add 2 teaspoons baking powder.

—Tipper Pressley

Tipper's Blueberry Pie

2 cups blueberries
2 tablespoon water
1 unbaked pie shell
½ stick butter
¾ cup sugar
1 tablespoon all-purpose flour
1 teaspoon cinnamon
½ teaspoon salt
1 egg slightly beaten

Place blueberries in a small saucepot with 2 tablespoons of water. Cook for 5 minutes with lid on, checking to make sure they don't scorch. Pour cooked blueberries and liquid into unbaked pie shell. Melt butter, remove from heat and stir in sugar, flour, cinnamon, salt and slightly beaten egg. Pour mixture over blueberries. Bake in a 350 oven for 35 minutes.

—Tipper Pressley

Strawberry Cobbler

1 stick butter
1 cup self-rising flour
1 cup sugar
1 cup milk

1 teaspoon vanilla
4 cups sliced strawberries (if strawberries are not very sweet,
toss with additional sugar)

Place butter in a 9" × 13" pan and put in oven. Preheat oven to 350 degrees. Mix together flour, sugar, milk and vanilla until smooth. Once butter is melted, pour flour mixture into pan. Do not stir. Spoon strawberries on top of flour mixture. Bake until crust has turned a golden brown—about 45 minutes.

NOTE: A wide array of berries and fruits lend themselves to this basic recipe. Among the berries are blackberries, raspberries, blueberries, gooseberries (will need more sugar), huckleberries and mulberries. Fruits that work include peaches, apples, firmer plums such as damsons and even figs.

—Jim Casada

Strawberry Pie

1 cup sugar
1 cup water
3 tablespoons cornstarch
3 tablespoons strawberry-flavored gelatin
2 cups sliced fresh strawberries
1 prebaked graham cracker pie shell

A strawberry pie with sliced berries shining on the top. *Tipper Pressley.*

Mix sugar, water and cornstarch and cook until thick and clear. Remove from heat. Stir strawberry gelatin into mixture. Place sliced strawberries into baked pie shell and pour sugar mixture over them. Chill pie until firm.

TIP: Brush graham cracker crust with egg and bake for 5 to 7 minutes at 375 degrees for a crisper crust.

—Tipper Pressley

Aunt Fay's Chocolate Cream Pie

I cup sugar
3 tablespoons all-purpose flour, sifted
3 tablespoons cornstarch
Pinch salt
⅓ cup cocoa
3 cups milk
I teaspoon vanilla
3 egg yolks, beaten; reserve egg whites for meringue
I prebaked 9-inch pie shell

Mix sugar, flour, cornstarch, salt and cocoa in a saucepot. Gradually add milk, stirring constantly. Cook over medium heat until mixture begins to thicken, stirring mixture often to prevent scorching. Once mixture has thickened, add a spoonful or two of it to egg yolks to temper them. Add tempered egg yolks back to pot and stir until mixture is very thick. Stir in vanilla, then beat the mixture—Aunt Fay said this makes the pie filling light and fluffy. Pour mixture into pie shell. To make meringue for the topping, beat egg whites with sugar to taste until peaks begin to form. At that point, spread the meringue atop the pie and then place it in the oven to brown. Keeping a close eye on it is essential because it can quickly turn from brown to burnt. Chill pie for several hours before serving.

NOTE: Whipped cream can be used in place of meringue.

TIP: Use additional egg whites for a fluffier meringue.

—Tipper Pressley

Pumpkin Pie
This traditional Thanksgiving dish was a fixture with the Casada family. We always had four or five choices of dessert, but this was one of my favorites. We grew our own pumpkins as well as cushaws, and the "meat" from the latter will also work in this recipe.

1 cup brown sugar
1 teaspoon ginger
1 teaspoon cinnamon
¼ teaspoon salt
1 cup stewed pumpkin
2 eggs, slightly beaten
2 cups milk
2 tablespoons melted butter
Pastry

Add the sugar and seasonings to the pumpkin and mix well. Then add the slightly beaten eggs and the milk. Lastly, stir in the melted butter. Turn into a pie plate lined with pastry and bake in a 425-degree oven for 5 minutes. Then lower the heat to 350 degrees and bake until the filling is set. The pie should be allowed to cool prior to serving.

—Jim Casada

Candy Roaster Pie

My granddaughter loves pumpkin pie, something that is a bit unusual in kids, and that consideration offers reason aplenty to make this pie from time to time.

¾ cup sugar
½ teaspoon salt
¼ teaspoon ginger
¼ teaspoon ground cloves
1 tablespoon cinnamon or pumpkin spice
2 large eggs
3 tablespoons maple syrup (use the real McCoy if you have it; if not, pancake syrup or even sorghum syrup will do)
1 cup cooked candy roaster flesh
1 (16-ounce) can evaporated milk
1 deep-dish pie shell (make your own or buy the 9-inch size at the grocery store)

Blend the dry ingredients and then, in a separate bowl, beat eggs before mixing syrup, candy roaster flesh and evaporated milk with them. Then gradually stir in the dry ingredients with a whisk until everything is thoroughly mixed. Pour into pie shell and bake in a preheated oven at 425 degrees for 12 minutes and then reduce heat to 350 degrees and bake until done (40 to 50 minutes). The pie is done when a knife or toothpick pulls away cleanly. The crust will have a tendency to get overly brown where exposed; this can be avoided by covering it with tinfoil. Cool on a pie rack before refrigerating or serving.

—Jim Casada

Anna Lou's Traditional Cobbler

Quickly prepared and simple, cobblers have long been a regional favorite. This simple approach will make the rankest of kitchen tyros a dessert star.

1 cup all-purpose flour
1 cup sugar
2 tablespoons baking powder
1 cup whole milk
1 stick butter or margarine, melted
2–4 cups blackberries

Preheat oven to 350 degrees. Combine flour, sugar, baking powder and milk; stir with a wire whisk until smooth. Add melted butter and whisk into batter. Pour batter into 9" x 13" baking dish. Pour berries (amount depends on personal preference and whether you like a lot of crust or mostly berries) evenly over the batter. Do not stir. Bake at 350 degrees for 30 to 40 minutes or until golden brown. Serves 6 to 8.

NOTE: While this recipe utilizes blackberries, it works equally well with about any type of fresh or frozen berry as well as cherries, peaches and apples.

TIP: For variety and a richer dessert, top a bowl of cobbler with a scoop of vanilla ice cream or half-and-half.

—Jim Casada

Summer Squash Pie

If you have squash (or zucchini) in such abundance the neighbors hide when they see you coming toting a suspicious-looking bag, here's a dessert option.

2 cups grated raw squash or zucchini
1 ½ cups sugar
3 eggs
½ stick butter
1 tablespoon flour
1 teaspoon lemon flavoring
1 teaspoon coconut flavoring
2 unbaked pie shells

Mix well and pour into pie shells. Bake for 45 minutes at 350 degrees.

—Jim Casada

Scuppernong Pie

1 ½ quarts scuppernongs or muscadines
¾ cup sugar
½ teaspoon almond flavor
½ stick real butter
1 tablespoon cornstarch
1 prebaked 9-inch pie shell

Squeeze pulp from ripe scuppernongs or muscadines and set seedy inside aside. Do this gently, in order to retain the juicy, sweet flesh attached to the hull, until you have a pint of hulls. Add sugar and stir into the hulls. Cook over gentle heat until tenderized, adding almond flavor and butter as you do so. Once tenderized, add cornstarch to thicken, and as mixture begins to cool, pour over pie shell. Allow to set and cool before slicing and serving.

TIP: The discarded inner pulp can be mashed through a sieve and used to make jelly.

—Jim Casada

Tipper and Aunt Fay's Butterscotch Pie

1 cup brown sugar
3 tablespoons all-purpose flour
3 tablespoons cornstarch
Pinch salt
3 cups milk
1 teaspoon vanilla
3 egg yolks, beaten; reserve whites for meringue
1 prebaked 9-inch pie shell

Mix brown sugar, flour, cornstarch and salt in a large pot. Gradually add milk while stirring constantly. Cook over medium heat until mixture begins to thicken, stirring often to prevent scorching. Once mixture has thickened, add a spoonful or two of it to the eggs to temper them. Add tempered eggs back to pot and stir until mixture is very thick. Stir in vanilla. Remove mixture from heat and beat well. Aunt Fay said beating the mixture makes the pie filling light and fluffy. Pour mixture into pie shell. To make meringue for the topping, beat egg whites with sugar to taste until peaks begin to form. At that point, spread the meringue atop the pie and then place it in the oven to brown. Keeping a close eye on it is essential because it can quickly turn from brown to burnt. Chill pie for several hours before serving.

NOTE: Whipped cream can be used in place of meringue.

TIP: Use additional egg whites for a fluffier meringue.

—Tipper Pressley

Chapter 25

COOKIES, BARS AND OTHER SWEETS

A cookie, or maybe several, with a glass of milk soothes the soul and feeds the hungry sweet tooth. Easily prepared, wonderfully suited to an array of nuts and always welcome as a quick snack, as a proper dessert, as gifts or during holidays, cookies, fruit or nut bars and similar small treats have universal appeal. In both our families, they were popular, prepared with regularity, often used as a little gift and always present around the holidays.

Oatmeal Krispies

1 ½ cups all-purpose flour
1 teaspoon salt
1 teaspoon baking soda
1 cup shortening
1 cup white sugar
1 cup brown sugar
2 eggs
1 teaspoon vanilla
3 cups quick-cooking oatmeal

Sift flour, salt and baking soda and set aside. Cream shortening with both sugars. Add eggs; mix well. Add vanilla; mix well. Add dry ingredients; mix well. Add oatmeal; mix well. Once you've completed these successive steps, roll dough into long rolls and wrap in foil or wax paper. Chill for at least 1 hour. Slice chilled rolls into ¼-inch slices. Bake at 400 for 6 to 8 minutes or until light brown.

TIP: Rolled cookie dough will last several days in refrigerator or may be frozen for future use.

—Tipper Pressley

Cherry Crisp

3–4 cups pitted cherries
1 cup sugar
1 cup all-purpose flour
½ cup oatmeal
1 teaspoon baking powder
1 teaspoon vanilla
1 egg
½ cup melted butter

Place cherries in a greased 9" × 13" baking dish. Mix sugar, flour, oatmeal, baking powder, vanilla and egg until crumbly. Sprinkle atop cherries. Dribble butter on top and bake at 400 degrees for 40 minutes.

TIP: Other fruit may be used in place of cherries.

NOTE: A scoop of vanilla ice cream takes this dessert up a notch.

—Tipper Pressley

Peach Bars
So very tasty! A really delicate crisp crust, and the peaches aren't overly sweet. Perfect with a cup of coffee or a glass of milk.

Dough
3 cups all-purpose flour
1 cup sugar
1 teaspoon baking powder
¼ teaspoon salt
1 cup (2 sticks) cold butter
1 egg

Filling
5 cups peeled and diced peaches
2 tablespoons lemon juice
½ cup all-purpose flour
1 cup sugar
¼ teaspoon salt
½ teaspoon cinnamon
¼ teaspoon nutmeg (optional)

To make dough, mix flour, sugar, baking powder and salt. Cut butter in using a pastry knife. Add egg and cut it into the dough. Divide dough in half. Pat half into a 9" x 13" baking pan. Place the other half along with the pan in the refrigerator while you prepare the filling.

To make filling, place peaches in a large bowl and gently mix in lemon juice. In a separate bowl, mix flour, sugar, salt, cinnamon and nutmeg. Pour over peaches and gently mix. Spread peach filling over chilled dough. Sprinkle remaining dough, which will be quite coarse and crumbly, on top, on top. Bake at 375 degrees for 45 to 50 minutes or until the top is lightly browned. Cool completely before serving.

—Tipper Pressley

Dollie's Black Walnut Cookies
Black walnuts are native to the Appalachian region and play a role in many traditional Appalachian desserts. This recipe has been handed down through generations of my husband's family back to his great-grandmother. That type of generational "pass it on" is typical of Appalachian foodways.

¾ cup shortening

A halved black walnut with meat waiting to be picked. *Tipper Pressley.*

2 cups brown sugar
2 eggs, beaten
1 cup black walnuts
1 teaspoon vanilla
3 cups all-purpose flour
½ teaspoon salt
½ teaspoon baking soda
½ cup evaporated milk

Cream shortening and sugar; add eggs and mix well. Mix in black walnuts and vanilla. In a separate bowl, sift flour, salt and baking soda together. Alternately add flour mixture and evaporated milk to sugar mixture. Beat vigorously. Drop teaspoon-size portions of dough onto greased cookie sheet and bake at 400 degrees for 7 to 10 minutes or until cookies are light golden brown.

NOTE: Cookie dough can be kept in the refrigerator and used as needed for up to two weeks.

—Tipper Pressley

Black Walnut Bars

Crust
½ cup butter
½ cup brown sugar, packed
1 cup flour

Filling
1 cup brown sugar
2 eggs, beaten
¼ teaspoon salt
1 teaspoon vanilla
2 teaspoons flour
½ teaspoon baking powder
1½ cups shredded coconut
1 cup black walnut meats

For the crust, cream butter and brown sugar. Slowly add flour and mix until crumbly. Pat into 7" × 11" baking dish. Bake for 8 to 10 minutes at 350 degrees until nicely browned.

For the filling, combine brown sugar, eggs, salt and vanilla. In a separate bowl, add flour and baking powder to coconut and walnuts. Blend into egg mixture and pour over baked crust. Return to oven and bake for an additional 15 to 20 minutes or until done. Cut into bars and place on wire racks to cool.

—Jim Casada

Oatmeal/Chocolate Chip/Walnut Cookies

1 ¼ cups butter, softened
½ cup granulated sugar
¾ cup light brown sugar, firmly packed
1 large egg
1 tablespoon vanilla extract
1 ½ cups all-purpose flour
1 teaspoon baking powder
½ teaspoon salt
3 cups quick-cooking oats
1 cup semisweet chocolate chips
¾ cup chopped and toasted black walnuts

Beat butter at medium speed with a mixer until creamy and gradually add sugars, beating well. Add egg and vanilla, beating until combined. Mix flour, baking powder and salt and then gradually add to the butter mixture, beating until blended. Stir in oats, chocolate chips and walnuts. Drop by rounded tablespoonfuls onto baking sheets. Bake at 375 degrees for 12 to 15 minutes or until lightly browned. Cool cookies on baking sheets for a minute and then remove to wire racks to cool completely.

—Jim Casada

Candy Roaster Cookies

A candy roaster is a type of squash once grown widely in Appalachia that is making a sort of modern comeback. It is an orange-pink color and cylindrical in shape. The flesh of a candy roaster is like that of a pumpkin, only it has a richer, sweeter taste.

⅓ cup shortening
1 ⅓ cups sugar
2 eggs
1 cup cooked candy roaster
1 teaspoon vanilla
1 teaspoon grated lemon rind
1 teaspoon lemon juice
¼ teaspoon ginger
¼ teaspoon allspice
1 teaspoon nutmeg
1 teaspoon cinnamon
1 cup raisins
½ cup chopped nuts (pecans, English walnuts and black walnuts are all suitable, but the latter nut has a delightfully distinctive taste)
2½ cups self-rising flour

Cream shortening and sugar and then add eggs one at a time, mixing well after each. Add candy roaster, vanilla, lemon rind, lemon juice, ginger, allspice, nutmeg and cinnamon. Mix well. Add raisins and nuts. Mix well. Add flour and mix until combined. Drop by rounded teaspoon onto a greased cookie sheet and bake at 400 degrees for 10 to 15 minutes or until golden brown. The cookies spread as they cook, so keep that in mind. These cookies are so good; every bite is like a taste of fall.

—Tipper Pressley

Chocolate No-Bake Cookies

These sweets are sometimes called Preacher Cookies, because they can be quickly made when the preacher shows up unexpectedly.

1 stick butter
½ cup milk
⅓ cup cocoa
2 cups sugar
1 teaspoon vanilla
½ cup peanut butter
3 cups one-minute oats (a little less for a
more chocolaty cookie)

Chocolate no-bake cookies.
Tipper Pressley.

Combine butter, milk, cocoa and sugar in a large saucepan over medium heat. Heat until boiling. Boil one minute. Remove from heat. Stir in vanilla and peanut butter. Once peanut butter has melted, stir in oats until thoroughly mixed. Drop by spoonfuls onto wax paper or aluminum foil.

—Tipper Pressley

Chapter 26

CANDY, SYRUPS AND SPECIAL TREATS

F rom taffy pullin' to molasses makin', from raising bees to the enduring temptation of properly made fudge, no coverage of what is sometimes lumped together as "sweet stuff" is complete without a brief glimpse at these treats for the sweet tooth.

Molasses making. *Courtesy of Hunter Library, Western Carolina University.*

Snow Cream

While most parts of the Appalachian South get at least some snowfall on an annual basis, a sho''nuff gollywhopper of a snow is another matter. When that occurs, one of the many rituals associated with it—along with snowball fights, sledding, building snowmen and the like—is enjoying snow cream. My mother turned into a kid on such occasions, and once depths reached four or five inches, she would say: "Let's make some snow cream." She would then send my siblings and me—or perhaps some of our friends, for whom the house always seemed to be operational headquarters, thanks in no small part to how well Momma cooked—outside with a dishpan. Our orders were to fill it up, using bowls or flour scoops, while being careful not to go too deep in the layer of snow covering the earth and get trash in the mix.

Once the pan was suitably full, a quick trip into the house, the addition of key ingredients and a bit of stirring produced the finished product. Here is Mom's basic recipe, although it can be expanded as needed.

1 cup whole milk or, for additional richness, half-and-half
½ cup sugar
½ teaspoon vanilla
Big bowl of snow (approximately 3 quarts)

The ingredients were stirred gently and consumed immediately. There were many variations to this basic recipe. The additional of chocolate syrup was popular, as was cocoa mix. For added richness, an egg could be beaten and stirred into the mix. Raisins soaked in water, drained and doused with a bit of rum flavoring offered another possibility. A dusting of cinnamon along with the aforementioned egg gave an eggnog-like taste. Frozen berries could be thawed and mixed in, or overripe bananas could be mashed up and added. Whatever the end product, it was always a special treat.

—Jim Casada

Popcorn Balls

Most mountain gardens of my youth included a couple of rows of popping corn, with its tight little cobs of strawberry-colored kernels that puffed up with a glorious symphony of noise when coated with a bit of grease and shaken in a popper over an open flame or a wood-burning stove. If you lack the real deal, and that's likely the case, store-bought popcorn will work just fine.

Popped corn, enough to make at least a dozen balls (pop plenty, because the extra amount can be eaten as is or even used to make an old-time Christmas tree decoration, strings of popcorn)
1 cup molasses, warmed
¼ stick butter
Pinch salt
1 tablespoon vanilla
Tetch (a small pinch) baking soda

Pop the corn as you normally would (but without adding any salt or butter). To make the syrup for the popcorn balls, warm the molasses with the butter and salt. Heat, stirring constantly, to boiling. At that point, add a spoonful of vanilla and "just a tetch" of baking soda and blend them in with more stirring before allowing the syrup to cool. Once the syrup mixture cools, pour it over a big mound of popcorn placed on wax paper atop a flat surface.

You are now ready to form the popcorn balls. In my experience, this has always been done with greased Number 8 pokes (for the uninitiated, that's mountain talk for paper bags) over your hands, but rubber gloves will do (just make sure they haven't been treated with talcum powder). Once gently rolled, shaped into a sphere roughly the size of a baseball and placed on cookie tins, some of the popcorn balls demand immediate consumption, while others will keep for a day or two as monuments to savory stickiness so sweet as to be irresistible. The whole process is a glorious mess and will eventually require liberal application of soap and warm water, once the whole production process is completed. Incidentally, young kids love making popcorn balls.

TIP: For interesting variety reminiscent of Cracker Jack, add toasted peanuts to the mix as the popcorn balls are being shaped.

—Jim Casada

Seaside Candy Roll

1 cup chopped pecans
⅓ cup butter, softened
⅓ cup corn syrup
1 teaspoon maple flavoring
½ teaspoon salt
4½ cups (1 pound) powdered sugar

Chop half of the pecans finely and the other half coarsely. Set the pecans aside in separate bowls. Mix together butter, corn syrup, maple flavoring and salt. Add powdered sugar a cup or so at a time, blending thoroughly until the mixture begins to resemble dough. Turn mixture out onto a board and knead in the rest of the powdered sugar and the finely chopped nuts. Once mixture is smooth, divide in half. Shape each half into a 2-inch-thick roll. Brush rolls with a little corn syrup and then roll in the coarsely chopped pecans. Wrap rolls in wax paper or foil and chill. Slice into ¼-inch pieces before serving.

—Tipper Pressley

Saltine Cracker Candy

1 sleeve saltine crackers (about 40)
1 cup brown sugar
1 cup butter
2 cups chocolate chips—dark, semisweet or milk chocolate, as you prefer
¾ cup chopped pecans

This recipe is really sticky, so make sure to line your cookie sheet with foil or parchment paper before placing the saltine crackers in a single layer atop it. It is also important to use a cookie sheet with at least ½ inch of lip on it to keep the brown sugar and butter from running off the edges.

Combine brown sugar and butter in a pot. Bring mixture to a boil and continue for 3 minutes. Quickly pour the brown sugar mixture over the crackers and spread evenly. Bake for 5 minutes in a 400-degree oven. This mixture will be quite bubbly at the end of 5 minutes. Sprinkle chocolate chips over crackers and let sit for a few minutes until the chips begin to melt. Spread melted chocolate chips over crackers and sprinkle on chopped pecans. Allow to cool completely. Break into pieces and store in an airtight container.

—Tipper Pressley

Buttermilk Pralines

It wouldn't be Christmas at the Pressley house without these rich pralines. They are perfect for the holiday season.

2 cups sugar
1 teaspoon baking soda
½ teaspoon salt
1 cup buttermilk
¾ cup butter
2 cups pecan halves or pieces
1 teaspoon vanilla

Combine sugar, baking soda, salt and buttermilk in a large saucepan and cook over high heat, stirring constantly until the mixture comes to a boil. Continue boiling and stirring until mixture begins to thicken and becomes slightly creamy (210 degrees on a candy thermometer). Add butter and pecans and continue boiling over medium-high heat until the candy thermometer reaches 234 degrees (soft ball stage).

Remove pan from heat and add vanilla. Allow mixture to cool about 2 minutes. Beat mixture until it begins to lose its gloss and becomes thick and creamy. Quickly, drop by spoonfuls in 2-inch rounds on waxed paper or foil to cool. If mixture becomes too hard, immerse the bottom of the pan in hot water for several minutes and resume dropping candy.

The hardest part of this recipe is knowing when to start dropping the pralines onto the paper. I've dropped too soon and ended up scraping it all up to cook a little more. The best advice I can offer, other than trial and error, is to pay close attention to the mixture. Honestly, these pralines are so good that even if I had to scrape the mixture back into the pan and cook a little longer every time I made them, it would be worthwhile. The pralines are creamy melt-in-your-mouth goodness.

—Tipper Pressley

Super Easy Black Walnut Fudge
Many fudge recipes are complex and time-consuming, but not this one.

12 ounces semisweet chocolate chips
1 (14-ounce) can sweetened condensed milk
1 teaspoon vanilla extract
½ cup black walnut meats

Line a 9" × 9" baking pan with wax paper, completely covering the bottom and sides, and have it in readiness. Place the chocolate chips (they must be semisweet, not milk chocolate) and sweetened condensed milk in a large bowl and microwave for 1 minute. Stir, making sure the chips melt completely, and if necessary, microwave a bit more. The chocolate needs to be smooth. Immediately stir in the vanilla and walnut meats and then transfer to the lined pan. Spread evenly and place in the refrigerator for at least 2 hours to set. Remove the fudge and cut into small squares once it has set and then store in an air-tight container. The fudge can be returned to the refrigerator or kept at room temperature. It will be softer if the latter approach is taken.

—Jim Casada

Homemade Long Sweetening

1 cup sugar
1 cup water

Mix and bring to a boil. Allow to cool and use to sweeten tea and other cold drinks. This recipe is a great way to save sugar, since it all dissolves in the water and none clumps in the bottom of the glass. By changing the ratios (4 parts water to 1 part sugar), it is also an ideal way to prepare hummingbird food.

—Tipper Pressley

Pancake Syrup

½ cup brown sugar
½ cup white sugar
½ cup water
¼ teaspoon maple flavoring (optional)
Pinch salt

Bring all ingredients to a boil and simmer until the liquid reaches the desired thickness.

—Tipper Pressley

Molasses Candy

Strictly speaking, it might be more accurate to call this sorghum syrup candy. But throughout the Appalachians, the word molasses, or sometimes just 'lasses, has long been employed to describe the syrup made from careful processing of juice from stalks of sorghum cane. Molasses making was a complex process involving many hands and requiring some special equipment, and the autumnal ritual was typically a community effort that, much like hog killing, combined an aura of celebration with plenty of hard work. It was all worth it in the end, because molasses was, for generations, the main mountain sweetening. Even today, a run of this candy harks back to festive fall days when this was one of many steps self-reliant folks took in preparing for winter. You will need a candy thermometer for this recipe.

1 cup molasses (or sorghum syrup)
1 cup sugar

Squeezing the juice from sorghum cane as a step in syrup production. *Courtesy of the National Park Service.*

2 tablespoons butter
1 ½ tablespoons apple cider vinegar
1 scant teaspoon baking soda

Butter two glass pie pans. In a large saucepan, stir together the molasses, sugar, butter and vinegar. Bring the mixture to a boil over medium-high heat, stirring steadily until it begins to boil. Continue to boil, without further stirring, until the syrup checks in at 265 degrees on your thermometer. At that point, stir in the baking soda and pour the mixture into the glass pans, dividing it evenly. Allow to cool until you can handle it (while still warm). Work with one batch at a time, pulling the candy into ropes, doubling over and pulling again. Continue this process until the candy shines and is golden in color and then stretch into a rope about ½ inch in width. Lay atop a cutting board and cut into 1-inch pieces with a knife or use kitchen scissors for the cutting. Allow to cool and store in plastic containers or wax paper–lined tins.

NOTE: If you have a helper—and grandkids love this kind of kitchen activity—you can work on both batches at the same time.

—Jim Casada

Chapter 27
TO QUENCH ONE'S THIRST

W hile nothing quite matches the elixir that is cold water from a mountain spring, Appalachian folks enjoy their cup of coffee of a morning as well as other beverages. That's especially true of those with a hint of sweetness. Here are a few, including a couple of old-timey ones, that fit the bill.

Granny's Hot Chocolate

½ tablespoon sugar
2 teaspoons cocoa
1 cup milk

Combine all ingredients in small pot and heat. Alternatively, make it in a microwave. Add sugar and cocoa to a cup. Stir in 1 tablespoon of hot water until smooth. Add milk, stir well and heat in a microwave.

—Tipper Pressley

Granny's hot chocolate.
Corie Graddick.

Russian Tea

At Christmas, Momma always made a big batch—or maybe two or three of them—of this seasonal delight. It was served at family gatherings, to visitors who just happened to drop by, at church functions and just as a refreshing hot drink on a cold winter's day.

½ teaspoon cloves
I cup sugar
½ teaspoon cinnamon
I gallon water
I tall can orange juice concentrate
Extra sugar, if desired

Bring these ingredients to a boil and continue for five minutes. Then add:

Pouring out a mug of Russian tea.
Tipper Pressley.

I pint tea (steep 4 tea bags in I pint of boiling water for 5 minutes)
¾ cup fresh lemon juice
I tall can (32 ounces) pineapple juice
I quart apple cider (optional)
I ½ cups fresh orange juice

The quantities of juice can be varied if you prefer one taste to another. This recipe will make 20 generous helpings, and leftovers can be stored in the refrigerator and reheated as desired. Grandpa Joe would sasser a piping hot cup of this (he called it "Rooshian" tea), slurp with obvious delight and declare, "My, that's some kind of fine."

—Jim Casada

❖ ❖ ❖

Float

I quart milk
4 large eggs
I cup sugar
2 teaspoons vanilla

Pour milk in a large saucepot and allow it to warm on medium heat. While milk is heating, mix eggs, sugar and vanilla in a bowl. Add part of the warm milk to the egg mixture to temper the eggs. Stir well and pour back in pot. Continue to stir and heat mixture until it reaches 175 degrees on a candy thermometer or until the mixture thickens slightly (it won't get very thick). If you end up with

Float. *Tipper Pressley.*

any scrambled egg pieces in the float, you can strain them out. Pour float in a jar and chill before serving.

TIP: A dusting of nutmeg can be sprinkled on top just before serving.

—Tipper Pressley

Birch Tea

In the spring of the year, tap a birch tree to extract the sap. It will be very clear and look like water. Combine sap with an equal amount of water and heat to boiling. Sweeten with sugar or honey. May be served hot or cold.

TIP: All birch tree sap is edible.

—Tipper Pressley

Maypop Tea

Maypops grow wild throughout the Appalachian Mountains. They are sometimes called wild apricots or passion fruits. They are best harvested when the green, egg-like outer covering or shell begins to fade in color and become wrinkled and soft. The fruit is easily harvested and is often eaten right where it grows by opening the hull and scooping out the sweet/tart goodness within. The pulp and seeds are both edible, although the seeds are rather crunchy. Young children in Appalachia have been known to stomp the fruit to hear the popping sound the fruit makes as it bursts.

To make maypop tea, scoop out pulp from ripe fruit and cook in water for 5 minutes. Strain and enjoy. Sugar may be added to water to increase the sweetness of the drink.

—Tipper Pressley

Lemonade

Lemons
Water
Sugar

Granny didn't make lemonade often, but when she did, the day seemed to be extra special. My brother Paul and I would run around the kitchen hurrahing and clapping for the cold, delicious beverage Granny set on the table for us.

When I first decided to make a pitcher of Granny's lemonade, I called her and asked for the recipe. She said: "Goodness, I don't have a recipe. Just bring some sugar and water to a boil, cut some lemons and put them in your pitcher, pour the sugar water over them, fill the pitcher the rest of the way with water, and let it sit for a while."

—Tipper Pressley

Mint Lemonade

Lemons
Sugar
Fresh sprigs of mint

Squeeze lemons, and if the fruit has seeds, run the juice through a sieve to remove them. Add to water and sweeten to taste. The refreshing

235

infusion of mint can be accomplished in two ways—by placing a number of bruised or gently crushed mint leaves in the pitcher holding the lemonade or by adorning each glass, as it is served, with a couple of leaves. That enables each individual to decide how much mint flavor they want.

—Jim Casada

Syllabub

Syllabub is an alcoholic beverage traditionally associated with Christmas and New Year's but suitable for festive occasions any time of the year. Its appearance definitely enhances the drink's appeal.

1 quart cream
½ pint sweet wine, with the peel of 2 lemons steeped in it for at least an hour (homemade elderberry wine has long been a favorite among old-time mountain folks and works well in making syllabub)
½ pint apple brandy (Madeira can be substituted)
Juice of 2 lemons (use peel to steep in wine)
Pinch powdered allspice
Sugar to taste

Whisk all the ingredients together in a large glass bowl, stirring vigorously until froth begins to rise. Skim away the froth, saving in a separate bowl, and continue whisking. Fill glasses halfway or a bit more with liquid and then top with froth. This is something of a novelty but is mighty tasty in the bargain.

—Jim Casada

Sassafras Tea

1 cup small sassafras roots, thoroughly washed and pounded with a meat hammer or similar tool until well broken up and yielding their spicy scent
½ cinnamon stick

6 cups cold water
3 tablespoons honey

Put the crushed roots and cinnamon in a saucepan with the water and bring to a rolling boil. Decrease the heat and simmer for fifteen minutes. Pour the tea through a fine strainer (cheesecloth topped by a coffee filter works just dandy) and then add the honey and stir it in. The beverage can be drunk hot or poured over crushed ice.

—Jim Casada

INDEX

W

Waldorf Salad 150
walnuts 40, 42, 43, 44, 45, 150,
      155, 195, 199, 200
  bars 219
  cookies 220
  Dollie's Black Walnut Cookies
      218
  English 43, 45, 197
  frosting 201
  pound cake 200
  Super Easy Fudge 228
water cress 139
watermelon 158, 159, 183
  Georgia Cannonballs 158
  with Salt 159
Watermelon Rind Pickles 183
Watermelon with Salt 159
wheat 21
whipped cream 156, 164, 166, 196
White Lily flour 34
wild plums 154
Wild Strawberry/Spinach Salad
      165
Wild Turkey Tenders 78
Williams, Aunt Mag 26
Wilson, Evelyn Louzine Jenkins
      "Granny" 5, 41, 105, 113,
      118, 159, 232, 235
Wilson, Jerry "Pap" 5, 27, 40, 159
Winter Squash and Kale 135
Worcestershire sauce 82, 83, 88

Y

Yuletide 199

Z

zucchini 38, 44, 132, 180, 181, 214
  bread 44
  pie 107

ABOUT THE AUTHORS

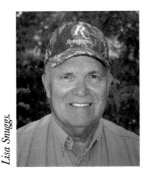

Lisa Snuggs.

Jim Casada is a former university professor who is now a full-time freelance writer. He is the author or editor of dozens of books and has published thousands of articles in regional and national magazines. Two of his most recent books are *A Smoky Mountain Boyhood* and *Fishing for Chickens: A Smokies Food Memoir.* Celebration of the folkways of his highland homeland has always been well to the forefront in his writing, and chronicling the region's culinary history figures prominently in his work. With his late wife, Ann, he coauthored seven cookbooks devoted to game, fish and other foods from the wilds. He writes a regular cooking column for *Smoky Mountain Living* magazine as well as featuring foodlore as a part of each one of his monthly e-newsletters. Over the course of his career, he has been the recipient of numerous awards for his books and other work.

Corie Graddick.

Tipper Pressley has been writing about all things Appalachian since 2008 on the popular blog *Blind Pig and the Acorn.* In 2020, she developed a YouTube channel, *Celebrating Appalachia,* to further solidify her desire to celebrate and preserve Appalachian culture. To date, over twenty million people have viewed her videos.

Foodways play a significant role in both endeavors. In addition to writing and filming, Tipper often teaches Appalachian cooking classes at locales throughout the region. She was awarded the 2020 e-Appalachia Award by the Appalachian Studies Association. In 2022, she received an Appy Award for her video work featuring Appalachian foodways, culture and heritage.

Visit us at
www.historypress.com
....